RACQUETE___

the Easy Way

RACQUETBALL
the Easy Way

Charles Garfinkel

ATHENEUM / SMI   *New York   1982*

PHOTOGRAPHS BY MICKEY OSTERREICHER
DIAGRAMS BY ELANA MILDENBERGER

Library of Congress Cataloging in Publication Data

Garfinkel, Charles.
    Racquetball the easy way.

    1. Racquetball.   I.   Title.
GV1017.R3G37 1978   796.34   78–53835
ISBN 0–689–70560–3

Copyright © 1978 by Charles Garfinkel
All rights reserved
Published simultaneously in Canada by
McClelland and Stewart Ltd.
Manufactured by
American Book-Stratford Press
Saddle Brook, N.J.
Designed by Kathleen Carey

First Printing November 1978
Second Printing January 1979
Third Printing November 1979
Fourth Printing June 1980
Fifth Printing September 1982

Dedication

To my dear wife Leslie for having extreme patience and good humor during the writing of this book.

To my children Bradley and Adina who have fully recovered from bruises received from the different shots that I practiced for the pictures in this book.

To my mother who has always been one of my biggest fans.

To my late father who would have been very proud of this book.

To Paul Smaldone and Bud Stange for their great help and support while writing this book.

To Barb Cornwall, Eddie Banck, Donna Meger, Bud, and Paul for appearing in the photographs in this book.

To Mickey Osterreicher for his superb photographs.

To Elana Mildenburger for her excellent diagrams.

To Mr. Dick Fischer, Al Litto & Racquet Club of Eastern Hills for their suggestions and use of their fine facility.

To Phillips Organisation and Frank Pace and Mike Hogan for their tremendous support and help with this book.

To Ektelon and Bud Held, Ron Grimes, Tom Stofko, Alana Klepper, and Peggy Watkins for their help over the years and their most appreciated involvement in *Racquetball the Easy Way*.

Contents

RACQUETBALL
the Easy Way

Racquetball–
Fun from the Start

RACQUETBALL IS THIS COUNTRY'S FASTEST-GROW-
ing sport.

Eight years ago there were about fifty-thousand
racquetball players in the United States. Today
there are nearly five million—and the game is really
just starting to boom. It already has a burgeoning
pro circuit with substantial tournament prize money
up for grabs.

All over the country, racquetball clubs are
being established at an incredible rate. In addition,
athletic clubs, YMCAs, Jewish Centers, and colleges
are building courts of their own. Men and women in
business, doctors and steelworkers, youngsters and
senior citizens—all sorts of people are taking up
racquetball.

Racquetball can be quickly learned by children and men or women of any age. In both the singles and doubles format of play, it provides lots of fun and challenge. Note in this view of a doubles match that the person hitting the ball is given plenty of room to do so by the other three players. It is against the rules to crowd or hinder another player's stroke.

What explains the sport's great popularity?

There are several reasons. The main one is that racquetball is fun to play *right from the start.*

The game is played with an eighteen-inch-long racquet that is easy to handle, and with a black rubber ball that is about the size of a tennis ball, only much livelier. These features permit beginners as well as experts to hit the ball many times during rallies.

Because the ball stays in play longer, you stay in motion longer and so get a better workout than you would in playing most other racquet sports. Only highly skilled tennis players or squash players really can extend themselves fully in an hour of playing those sports, for example. But after an hour or so on the racquetball court, even the novice can feel pleasantly exhausted.

In addition to being such a fun game, racquetball is an excellent sport to play in order to remain physically fit. You can practice on a court by yourself and still get a full workout.

In singles, you'll greatly enjoy playing against another person at your own level. Even if you are both novices, you'll still get a tremendous workout.

In doubles, where you have two teams of two persons each, you will find that you can play for a longer period of time because you don't have to cover as much of the court. Doubles is becoming increasingly popular in racquetball because it gives entire families and small groups of friends a chance to have fun together.

Another reason racquetball is growing so rapidly is that it is convenient to play. With all the new courts going up, people can schedule their matches or practice sessions for almost any time of day. Many clubs are open from 6:00 A.M. to midnight, seven days a week. And you never have to worry about being rained out in racquetball—courts are always fully enclosed, since the ceiling of the court is an integral part of the game.

Finally, racquetball is inexpensive to play. Equipment and clothing need not cost much, and there is a wide range of membership fees available at racquetball clubs. A single person can join a club for as low as $25, with the cost of court-time running an additional $2.50–$5.00 per hour, depending on the time he or she wants to play. If you belong to a YMCA or a Jewish Center, it may be even less expensive to play—although court time at these places may be somewhat harder to come by.

Racquetball had its beginnings in Greenwich, Connecticut, back in 1950. Joe Sobek left his position as tennis and squash pro for a desk job, and the local YMCA became his main outlet for physical activity. He tried paddleball and handball. The paddleball racquet was very cumbersome and the handball hurt his hands. (Although handball and racquetball have the same rules and are played on

A long and varied exchange of shots, as shown in the sequence on these pages, is typical of how a point is played in racquetball. The different shots and tactics used in this exchange are explained in detail in later chapters.

Server puts ball in play.

Receiver returns ball to the front wall.

Server races back to take ball on his forehand and return shot to front wall.

Receiver is forced to hit defensive shot on ball that has come very close to sidewall.

Server attacks with hard shot to front wall.

Receiver is forced to return this shot from a cramped position deep in the court.

Server takes advantage of receiver's not watching him to hit ball sharply crosscourt instead of back down the line.

Change in pattern of play catches the receiver out of position and he barely returns ball to front wall.

Server now hits a high ball to change the pace of rally in progress and further disrupt opponent.

Receiver, forced into deep right corner, has not had time to get completely set to hit his shot.

Server exploits the weak return and hits an unreturnable "roll-out"—a ball that comes off the wall so low to the floor that opponent can't get his racquet on it.

identical courts, the handballs are much smaller and livelier than racquetballs. You must also be adept with both hands to play handball.)

Sobek then designed his own racquet, with one major difference from the paddleball racquet. The dimensions were the same, but his racquet had strings, whereas the paddleball racquet was completely solid. The new racquets looked like sawed-off tennis racquets.

After experimenting with different balls, Sobek got a manufacturer to make some racquetballs that he felt were well suited for the game. Although the balls were low-bouncing by today's standards, Sobek's friends at the Greenwich YMCA readily took to the new game.

The game slowly grew and had its first national tournament in 1969. At this time, the International Racquetball Organization was formed.

In 1973 the IRA had a split in the top levels of the organization. A new, rival organization called the National Racquetball Club was formed. At first the IRA was strictly amateur and the NRC strictly pro. Today both are involved in amateur and professional racquetball alike.

Professional racquetball is booming, but the game is still geared toward the everyday player.

How Racquetball
Is Played

RACQUETBALL IS PLAYED INSIDE A FOUR-WALL IN-
door court that is twenty feet wide, twenty feet high
and forty feet long. The back wall must be at least
twelve feet high.

Some courts have glass sidewalls or back walls,
which permit spectators to watch matches. Most
court walls are made of cement blocks covered with
plaster. Other courts are paneled.

A match between two players (or teams) con-
sists of a best-of-three series of games. In the most
popular scoring system in use today, the first two
games are played to 21 points. If each player wins a
21-point game, then a third game, called a tie-
breaker, is required. The tiebreaker game is played
to 11 points.

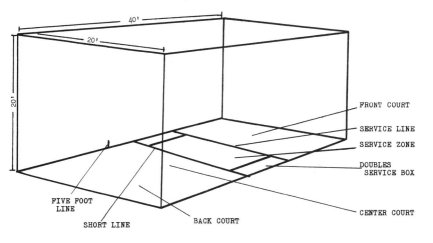

This diagram shows the standard racquetball court, giving its dimensions and the names for the significant parts of the playing area.

In racquetball, a player can only score a point on his or her own serve. There is no "deuce" scoring, as exists in other racquet sports. If a game reaches 20–20, the very next point decides the winner of the game.

At the outset of a match, players determine who will have the advantage of serving first by flipping a coin, or some similar method. If a third game is necessary to settle the match, then the player who has scored the most points in the first two games is entitled to serve first.

To begin play, the server stands in the serving zone, a five-foot-deep area marked with lines in the front half of the court. The line nearest the front wall is called the *service* line. The line nearest the back wall is called the *short* line.

Server and receiver in position prior to the start of a point. Server is at or near the center of the service zone. Receiver is deep in the backcourt. Prior to putting ball into play, server should check receiver's position, as this alone may dictate a special serving strategy.

The two small lines forming a box near each sidewall are strictly for doubles. In doubles, when your partner is serving, you must stand in either box until the serve has crossed the short line.

Another line put on some courts is a little red mark five feet back from the short line. It is placed on both sidewalls as a safety feature. The receiver cannot cross this line until the served ball has crossed the short line. This prevents the receiver from rushing into the service zone and perhaps colliding with or causing injury to the server.

The server must have both feet positioned in the serving zone. He has up to ten seconds in which to serve the ball. The receiver must stand behind the short line in the backcourt. The server must remain in the serving area until the ball passes the short line.

To serve, a player bounces the ball on the floor and hits it so that it strikes the front wall first, and on the rebound hits the floor in back of the short line, either with or without touching a sidewall. If after hitting the front wall, the serve bounces and hits both sidewalls, the back wall, or the ceiling, it is considered a fault. Two faults result in a loss of serve.

The server must also be sure not to "screen" his serve. This happens when the ball rebounds off the front wall and passes within eighteen inches of the server's body. This is called a screen serve because the server's body blocks the ball from the view of the receiver. The server must play the point over, even if he had hit a good serve.

SCREENING FAULT ON SERVE. *Server has allowed ball to pass too close to his body, thus "screening" the action and preventing receiver from getting a clear view of the serve. Point must be played over.*

The opponent must return the ball to the front wall, but he can hit any combination of walls, including the ceiling, to get the ball to the front wall. The opponent may take the serve in the air or on the bounce, but he must wait until the ball passes the short line.

As long as the ball does not hit the floor before it hits the front wall, it is a good shot. If, however, a shot hits the front wall and then rebounds over the back wall and out of court on the fly, the point is played over.

The game is on! Each player keeps returning the ball to the front wall until one player cannot return the ball properly. This would occur when a player lets the ball bounce on the floor more than once before returning it, or produces a shot that hits the floor before it hits the front wall.

If the server's opponent misses a shot, the server wins a point, and serves again. If the server misses a shot (including double-faulting), he gives up the advantage of the serve to the opponent.

Once the ball is in play, you and your opponent will be trying everything within legal limits to win the rally. Usually, the player that controls the center of the court in the area near the short line should win the rally. By being in this position, you are never very far from any shot that is hit by your opponent. You will be able to anticipate where the ball is going by looking behind you as your opponent starts to hit the ball.

19

CORRECT. *Player gives opponent plenty of room to hit his shot.*

INCORRECT. *Player obstructs opponent, making it difficult for opponent to make a shot. Opponent is entitled to call interference when this happens, and under the rules win point or regain serve.*

Even though you want to win, make sure to play fairly. This means giving your opponent a clean shot at the ball whenever it is his turn to hit. According to the rules, if you block your opponent's shot or get in his way as he tries to move to the ball, you stand to lose the point on your serve.

What makes rallies so much fun are the wild caroms and bounces that can occur. The ball may hit the wall in such a way that it will ricochet crazily or jump up at your opponent.

The more skilled you are, the lower you will try to hit the ball on the front wall. It is a great thrill to see your own shot roll out—hit the front wall so low that it rolls along the floor without bouncing. Frustration abounds when you are all set to hit a ball close to the sidewall, and you wind up just hitting the wall.

Getting Equipped
for Racquetball

THE PROPER EQUIPMENT FOR RACQUETBALL IS INEX-
pensive and relatively easy to acquire, but you
should know what you're shopping for. Racquetball
clubs and many sporting-goods stores now have
well-stocked pro shops and racquetball depart-
ments, staffed by people who can answer any specific questions you may have. Here are some general
guidelines.

RACQUETS

If you have played a lot of tennis, forget about all
the theories you have heard on racquets in that
sport.

The main types of racquets available for playing racquetball are pictured here: (from left to right) fiberglass, aluminum, wood and graphite. All racquets come equipped with wrist thong as safety measure.

In tennis, for example, it is commonly thought that wood gives you more control, while metal helps the ball move off the racquet more quickly. But in racquetball, wooden racquets are not recommended. In fact, in some courts they are forbidden because of the damage they can do to walls. Besides that, wooden racquets are too cumbersome and cannot be swung quickly enough.

Plastic and fiberglass racquets tend to vibrate and fail to absorb shock well. Both wood and plastic racquets can give you "tennis elbow." The new graphite racquets give you a good "feel," but they do not yet respond as well as aluminum racquets do. Good aluminum racquets are the best choice for racquetball. The feel of a good aluminum racquet is unmistakable. You get a well-hit ball with every swing. Even if you hit the ball near the top or the bottom of the strings, you still make a solid hit. With the best aluminum racquets, you get a year's guarantee on the frame and a ninety-day guarantee on the strings.

Racquet frames vary in flexibility, or "flex." A more flexible racquet "gives" greatly when you are hitting the ball, creating a good feeling of control. A firmer racquet-frame may provide more power but could also cause some elbow problems.

Racquets vary in length from $17\frac{1}{2}$–19 inches. Generally speaking, most junior and women players prefer racquets that are $17\frac{1}{2}$–18 inches long. These shorter racquets are easier to maneuver and also more flexible. Most men tend to use $18^1/_2$–19-inch-long racquets. A strong, hard, powerful player also will want a racquet that is stiffer. Personal preference still enters greatly into the player's final choice.

All racquets come equipped with a string, or lanyard, securely attached to the bottom of the handle and looped around the player's wrist during a match as a safety measure.

RACQUET WEIGHT

Racquets generally weigh beyween $8^1/_2$ and 9 ounces. Women and junior players generally prefer racquets between $8^1/_2$ and 9 ounces. Men players prefer the heavier weights, between 9 and $9^1/_2$ ounces.

Racquets that are too heavy can cause elbow problems. You will not be able to swing at the ball as quickly and you will have a tendency to mis-hit the shot. Racquets that are too light will not give you the feeling of a really solid hit when you make contact with the ball, as they will tend to vibrate.

Before buying your first racquet, swing several samples to see how light or heavy they feel to you. Most pro shops or sporting-goods stores also have special scales for checking the weight of specific racquets.

RACQUET GRIP SIZE

Most racquet handles range in diameter from $3^{15}/_{16}$ inches to $4^1/_8$ inches for juniors and women

CORRECT GRIP SIZE. *To find the racquet suited to your own hand, grip various racquet handles until you locate one that leaves only a small amount of space between your fourth finger and your thumb.*

GRIP SIZE TOO SMALL. *If fingers overlap, the racquet handle is too small in diameter for your hand.*

GRIP SIZE TOO LARGE. *If there is considerable space between your fourth finger and thumb, the racquet handle is too fat for your hand.*

players and from $4^5/_{16}$ inches to $4^1/_2$ inches for men players. It's important to select a racquet with the correct grip size for your hand. Otherwise, it could slip or turn in your hands.

To find your correct grip size, wrap your hand around the racquet, then check the space remaining between your thumb and your fourth finger. If the space is too wide, the racquet is too big for you. If your fingers overlap, the racquet is too small.

RACQUET STRINGS

In tennis, expensive gut-stringing is preferred by many players because it aids in "feel" and in ball control. In racquetball, however, top-grade nylon stringing does the job at a much lower cost. In racquetball, the ball does not grab as tightly on the racquet, so the roughness of gut-stringing would serve no purpose.

For the best ball control, most players should use racquets strung with 22–28 pounds tension. Most women and juniors should have their racquets strung with 22–24 pounds tension. Most men should have their racquets strung with 25–28 pounds.

If a racquet is strung higher than 28 pounds, even a strong player may not feel real control of the shot. It will feel as if you are hitting the ball with a board.

If you are an advanced player, you may want to buy a racquet that has not been strung. That way you'll be able to have the racquet strung exactly at the tension you want.

Many players prefer leather grips on their racquet handles, because they feel more natural. They are also easier to grip firmly, and are less likely to cause blisters. Less-expensive rubber grips are also popular, but they tend to slip more in your hand.

GLOVES

Many players wear lightweight leather gloves on their hitting hands to help them hold onto the racquet better. Other players contend that you get a better "feel" and more racquet control with your bare hand. Players who perspire greatly will tend to have more trouble with the racquet slipping in their hands, and so should definitely consider buying gloves.

RACQUETBALLS

Racquetballs are sold in pressurized cans, two to a can. Don't buy balls that do not come in such cans, as they will not be as lively or as long-lasting. When you open a new can, listen for that "fizz" of air escaping, which will indicate the balls are indeed fresh.

Fresh, lively balls are easier and more enjoyable to play with. Hitting dead balls for long periods can cause unnecessary strain and stress on your arm.

Most racquetballs cost about $3.00 for a can of two. A ball should stay lively for an hour's workout. It may also be good for a second hour's workout. After that you should use a new ball.

Always store racquetballs in your house—never leave them in a car or a cold place. Low temperatures deaden the bounce.

SNEAKERS

Next to racquet and balls, sneakers are the most important pieces of equipment in racquetball. A good pair of low-cut, lightweight sneakers will not only provide better support and protection for your feet, but also will help you move more quickly on the court. Some players prefer wearing the high-top sneakers for added support. Whatever kind you choose, be sure to wear good-quality footwear.

SOCKS

If you wear two pairs of socks when you play, it will cut down on blisters and other foot problems. Wear thick wool socks over light cotton socks.

APPAREL

You don't have to wear tennis outfits or fancy warm-up suits for racquetball, though these are perfectly suitable. A clean T-shirt and a pair of gym shorts that fit snugly at the waist and allow plenty of room at the hips and thighs will do fine.

WRIST- AND HEAD-BANDS

These items keep perspiration from getting into your eyes and on your hands. I recommend the use of the adjustable headband rather than the elastic stretch variety, which can sometimes cause headaches.

EYEGLASS HOLDERS

Eyeglass holders are important for those players who wear glasses. Even though you wear glasses that fit snugly, I strongly urge that you also obtain eyeglass holders. Glass- and eye-protectors are also available. They provide added protection for those players who wear glasses and for players who wish to have their eyes shielded.

Forehand Grip
and Stroke

IN RACQUETBALL, THE CORRECT FOREHAND AND backhand grips enable you to make contact with the ball effectively—and without running the risk of hurting your arm. An improper grip may lead to a case of "tennis elbow," or pulled or torn muscles in the wrist or shoulder.

To acquire the correct forehand grip, hold the racquet in your left hand at the throat (left-handers must read "right" for "left" throughout these instructions). Now shake hands with the racquet handle with your right hand. Your hand should wrap snugly and comfortably around the handle of the racquet. Your fingers should be spread apart slightly.

Another way to establish the correct forehand

31

FOREHAND GRIP. *To obtain a good forehand grip, "shake hands" with the racquet as shown. Or, place your hitting hand palm down on the racquet strings, slide the hand down to the racquet, then wrap fingers around handle.*

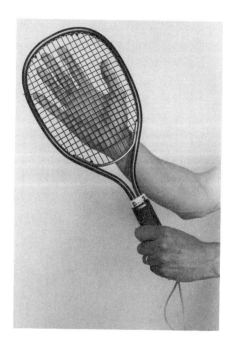

CORRECT. *Fingers are slightly spread apart on the handle. This provides more "feel" for stroking and greater power on shots.*

INCORRECT. *When fingers are tightly clenched, there is less freedom of movement in making strokes. Also, this overly tight grip can lead to cramps in the hand and forearm.*

grip is to hold the racquet in your left hand once again, and then spread the open fingers of your right hand on the racquet strings. Now slide that hand down from the racquet face to the handle. Your hand will come to rest wrapped around the handle in a manner similar to that described in the previous paragraph.

Some players complain that their hands feel cramped after playing. This may be the result of having their fingers too close together on the handle, or continually holding the racquet too tightly. When you are waiting to hit the ball, you should hold the racquet in a relaxed manner. When you are making contact with the ball, you should hold the racquet firmly. Keeping your fingers slightly spread apart on the handle allows you to grip it comfortably and effectively.

MAKING THE FOREHAND STROKE

The forehand stroke is the workhorse shot in racquetball. It is used in modified form to serve the ball, as well as to return balls hit to the right side of the body. So it's vital to learn the stroke properly.

Get acquainted with the basics of the forehand stroke during a practice session with a racquetball pro, or at least with an experienced player who will be patient enough to "feed" you balls to the forehand side.

READY POSITION. *In a good ready position, player is relaxed, in good balance with knees bent, and prepared to move quickly for the ball in any direction. Racquet is held in front with both hands. The hitting hand is in the forehand grip; the free hand will hold the racquet in case it is necessary to shift to the backhand grip quickly.*

In preparing to make the stroke, stand in a comfortable "ready" position, with both hands on the racquet. The racquet head should be slightly raised, rather than dropped low in front of you. This permits you to start your backswing more quickly. The left hand (right hand for lefties, remember) is positioned on the handle to help you turn your racquet to the backhand grip when necessary, as we'll see later.

Your body should be in a slight crouch. Make sure your knees are bent. That way you'll be ready for any shot that comes. Your opponent will be trying to produce shots that make you move, so the better the starting position you're in, the more easily you'll win the race to get to the shot that your opponent has produced.

The ready position is a posture you should return to after every shot you make, if you have the time.

Now for the stroke itself:

When you see the ball coming in your direction from the front wall, turn your body to the right side, drop your left hand from the racquet handle—holding it out in the air toward the front wall to help your balance—and bring your racquet up over your head. This high backswing differs from the low backswing used in tennis. In tennis, you don't need the high backswing because the racquet is much heavier and longer. In racquetball, the high backswing helps you hit the ball with much more power and control.

At this point, you will be in a stance that is quite similar to that of the batter in baseball who has just seen the ball released from the pitcher's fingers. The racquet is held high behind you in relation to the oncoming ball, just as the baseball player holds his bat high behind him in relation to the pitch.

To start the forward swing, your knees should bend slightly and your weight should shift forward onto the front foot. Now the racquet moves on a slight high-to-low plane into the ball.

Be sure to keep your eyes focused on the ball at this time. You should try to see the ball hit the strings as you make contact slightly in front of your front foot.

Your hitting arm will naturally straighten as you make contact with the ball. The racquet face moves through the hitting area and slightly under the ball. This will produce underspin. This is very important, because it makes the ball stay very low after it hits low on the front wall. (Topspin is not desirable in racquetball, because it causes the ball to rise slightly.)

After contact, the racquet follows through to a high finish position. The high follow-through assures you of more power and better control on this stroke.

Your aiming point in first practicing the forehand should be a spot 3–5 feet high on the front wall. As you progress and gain more confidence in your game, you can start putting your forehands lower and lower on the front wall.

THE FOREHAND IN ACTION

Player turns sideways to prepare for his shot and carefully watches ball as it approaches.

Racquet is held high on backswing. Player steps toward ball with front foot to maintain balance.

Knees remain bent ensuring that player will remain low to the oncoming shot.

Ideal contact point is off the front foot.

After contact, racquet moves upward, a sign that good control has been achieved on shot.

In proper finish, racquet finishes high and in front of opposite shoulder. Free arm naturally extends for balance.

Here's a summary of the main points on the forehand stroke:

1. Be in a good ready position.
2. Have the proper forehand grip.
3. Turn your body to the right side the moment you see that the ball is coming that way.
4. Bring your racquet back to a high position.
5. Start your forward swing, stepping toward the ball.
6. Keep your eyes on the ball at all times.
7. Strike the ball slightly in front of you.
8. Continue your forward swing in the direction of the spot on the front wall that you want your shot to strike.
9. Follow through to a high position—just as high as your backswing racquet-position.
10. Quickly return to your ready position in preparation for your opponent's next shot.

PRACTICING THE FOREHAND

The best way for beginners to practice the forehand is in a session with a qualified pro or a good, experienced player. It's better to groove your basic forehand this way than to try to do so during actual competition.

Your practice partner should stand on the backhand side of the court (left side), a few feet be-

TOO CLOSE TO SIDEWALL. *Player has jammed himself by getting too close to a ball that has come off the sidewall. It will be almost impossible for him to return the ball to the front wall.*

PROPER DISTANCE FROM SIDEWALL. *By quickly moving away from the sidewall in anticipation of the shot, player has put himself in position to execute a normal forehand.*

hind the short line, and feed shots to you, standing on the forehand side at about the same depth.

Try to hit the ball with a nice, easy, fluid swing, driving it to a spot on the front wall 3–5 feet from the floor. Try to keep the balls off the sidewalls and back wall at first. Also, make sure that you move out of your helper's way so that he will have plenty of room to hit his shot. You are merely trying to establish a "feel" for the shot. You are not trying to see how hard and low you can hit it on the front wall.

As you gain more confidence in your shots, have your partner give you shots that come off the front wall faster. Return these shots by hitting as hard as feels comfortable to you.

Once you feel that your confidence is growing greatly on shots hit off the front wall, your partner should start giving you shots that hit the right sidewall after hitting the front wall. This will help you adapt to the various angles at which the ball will come off the sidewalls. In preparing to take balls off the sidewall, you'll have to move more away from the sidewall in order to have room to take a full stroke at the ball.

As you gain confidence in returning these shots off the sidewall, have your partner increase the speed of his shot. If you are having difficulty, have him slow it down.

Next, your partner should give you shots that hit the front wall, bounce, and then rebound off the back wall. As before, start slowly and then increase

EXTRA-LOW FOREHAND. *To play a shot below knee level, player must bend fully to make sure hitting hand and racquet head remain on the same level at the time of contact.*

the speed of the shots.

Once you feel that you have mastered these different angles and shots, you may try to hit the ball lower on the front wall. Two things will enable you to produce lower shots: (1) letting the ball drop lower before you hit it, and (2) bending much lower as you hit the shot.

Practice as many shots as you can, over and over again, on your forehand side. A half-hour session will give you a good feeling for the dynamics of the shot and the variety of ways in which it plays inside the racquetball court. But it will take several good practice sessions for most newcomers to the game to really groove the forehand stroke in all its different applications.

Backhand Grip
and Stroke

You may rely on your forehand a great deal in racquetball, but you'll never be a complete player unless you also have a good backhand.

Most players have problems with their backhand because they attempt to execute it with a forehand-type grip. Not only does this grip produce a weaker breed of backhand shot, it also leads to unnecessary strain on the hitting arm, particularly the elbow.

To obtain the correct backhand grip, stand in the ready position and assume your good forehand grip. Now move the racquet a quarter-turn to the left (counter-clockwise) That's all there's to it. Note that your fingers are spread on the racket handle, just as they are in the forehand grip—they are de-

BACKHAND GRIP. *Looking down on the racquet as though from the player's view, observe that the hand is more on top of the handle than it is for the forehand grip. The V formed by thumb and forefinger is lined up on the left edge of the racquet handle. For the forehand grip it would be lined up more on the right edge.*

finitely not in a clenched-fist position.

Exact thumb position in the backhand grip varies from player to player. You may keep your thumb along the back of the handle, or you may wrap it around the handle. In my experience, positioning the thumb along the handle allows greater control over shots. But by all means experiment.

There are two acceptable ways to position the thumb in the backhand grip.

THUMB UP THE HANDLE. *Most players find this thumb position provides greater control.*

THUMB WRAPPED AROUND HANDLE. *Some players prefer to hit their backhands with the thumb wrapped around, as shown, and are able to do so without sacrificing control.*

MAKING THE BACKHAND STROKE

Stand in your ready position, both hands on the racquet, facing the front wall.

As you see the ball approaching, turn your body to the left side and raise your racquet high. Make sure your right shoulder pivots completely sideways. This will allow more freedom of movement in your swing.

As you start the forward swing, your right foot steps toward the oncoming ball. Upon contact with the ball slightly in front of you, your hitting arm straightens and the racquet moves slightly under the ball, producing underspin. The racquet continues to swing through the ball and finishes high.

Here's a summary of the main points to remember when practicing the backhand:

1. Be in a good ready position.
2. Switch to your backhand grip the moment you see the ball is coming to the left side of your body.
3. Turn your body sideways to the front wall.
4. Bring your racquet back to a high position on the backswing.
5. Start your forward swing and step forward at the same time.
6. Keep your eyes on the ball at all times.
7. Meet the ball in front of your front leg.

THE BACKHAND IN ACTION

As ball approaches, player turns sideways and takes racquet back. He has already shifted from a forehand grip to the backhand grip.

Racquet is brought back high on the backswing. Player steps out toward ball with front foot.

Player bends knees and watches ball closely as he brings racquet forward.

Contact is made slightly in front of the lead foot.

After contact, racquet continues forward and up.

High finish denotes maximum power and control.

8. Swing through the ball and out toward the spot on the front wall that you want the ball to strike.
9. Follow through to a high position.
10. Immediately get ready for the next shot.

PRACTICING THE BACKHAND

As with the forehand, I would recommend that someone help you practice the backhand on a court, when you are free of competitive concerns. You should hit many shots over and over with your backhand. Don't try to put the ball away with an extra-forceful stroke during the beginning sessions. Concentrate instead on taking a nice, fluid swing and making a full follow-through. As you gain confidence, continue practicing as you did on the forehand.

PRACTICING FOREHAND AND BACKHAND TOGETHER

How do you switch grips fast enough from the forehand to the backhand, or vice versa, during a rally?

I suggest standing in front of a full-length mirror at home. Assume your ready position with a forehand grip. Go through the complete forehand swing and then return to the ready position. Now prepare to make the swing for a backhand shot. Note that in the ready position, your left hand is on the throat of the racquet and your right hand is on the handle. As you start to bring your racquet back to hit the backhand, change your grip by shifting the position of your hand a quarter-turn to the left. Do this a number of times until you can change grips quickly and comfortably.

Now, when practicing with your pro or helper, ask him or her to alternate shots to your forehand and backhand. This will force you to move about the court more in establishing proper hitting stances. Even though the shots your practice partner feeds you will be relatively easy to hit, you will be getting a much better awareness of actual game conditions, and you will gain valuable experience in changing back and forth between grips. You will also be gaining confidence in both your forehand and backhand strokes, and in the special timing required to hit them both effectively.

As you gain confidence, you can continue to practice all of the harder shots in this way.

Serving

THE ONLY TIME YOU CAN SCORE POINTS IN RACQUET-
ball is when you are serving, so obviously it's important to obtain the serving advantage and to serve
well when you have it. An effective server can completely control play and thoroughly frustrate opponents.

To put the ball into play, the server must stand
with both feet inside the five-foot-deep serving zone,
or box. The opponent can stand anywhere in the
backcourt behind this area.

The serve is made by letting the ball bounce,
then hitting it against the front wall with enough
force to cause it to bounce on the floor somewhere in
the backcourt beyond the serving zone. If the ball
fails to reach the backcourt area before bouncing—

if it hits the floor short of the short line or within the service box—it counts as a fault. It is also a fault if the ball hits the front wall and then rebounds on the fly off the back wall without bouncing first.

The serve may strike one sidewall in rebounding off the front wall on its way to the backcourt. But if it should strike two sidewalls before bouncing, that also counts as a fault.

In preparing to serve, you have ten seconds in which to serve the ball. Just before bouncing the ball to serve, you should turn and look at the receiver. This will let him know that you are ready to play, and also that you are aware of where he is standing. You may detect him leaning to the right or left side, which means that you could serve a hard serve to the opposite side for an easy point. You then must bounce the ball before putting it into play. A variety of markedly different serves can be produced by varying such things as where you stand in the service box, the height at which you bounce the ball, the force of your actual swing, and the spot on the front wall to which you direct the serve. The more experienced you become, the more control you'll have over these factors and the more versatile and effective your serving will become.

There are four main types of racquetball serves—the drive serve, the lob serve, the garbage (or low-lob) serve, and the Z-serve. All are made with variations of the basic forehand stroke, so the racquet should be held in the forehand grip for all of them.

There are a minority of players who serve with a backhand grip. They do this because they have more confidence in their backhand than their forehand. They cannot, however, get the control or power that their forehand would generate. Their bodies face away more from the front wall, and so they can be passed much more easily on the return of serve.

THE DRIVE SERVE

The drive serve has become especially effective ever since the introduction of livelier balls to the sport a few years ago. You are more likely to get an unusual bounce off the sidewall or back wall when serving because of the higher speeds possible with the newer balls. Some players blast their serves past their opponents without hitting any wall.

On the drive serve, your goal is to hit the ball hard and low so that it flies deep into a backcourt corner without hitting the sidewall or back wall. The lower the ball remains, the harder it will be for the opponent to return.

To hit the drive serve, stand sideways to the front wall in a low crouch in the middle of the serving zone. Visualize a target on the front wall about three feet off the floor and one foot to the right of center (or nine feet from the right sidewall). If you direct the ball to this spot with sufficient force, it will

THE BASIC DRIVE SERVE

*This serve is most effective when it is kept low and hit deeply
into one of the far back corners of the court, as shown in
diagram.*

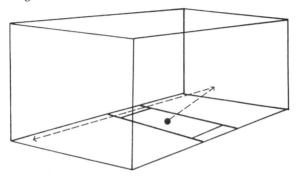

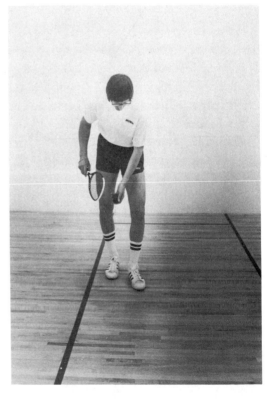

*Player has checked opponent's position in backcourt and is
ready to serve from a position midway in the service zone.
Note balance and concentration.*

Server brings racquet back high as he tosses ball to the right.

Server stays low as he steps toward the ball.

Ball is met well below knee level to make sure serve stays low.

Server strokes through ball, rather than falling back immediately.

High followthrough maximizes serving power. Player now must take note of opponent's actions and assume a good ready position.

rebound deep into the right corner, or the receiver's forehand side (assuming your opponent is right-handed). Change your target area to a spot one foot to the left of center, and your drive will rebound deep into the left corner, or the receiver's backhand side. Since many players' backhands are their weaker shot, this may be the preferred serving strategy.

To start the serve, let the ball drop in front of your lead foot and bounce up no higher than knee-level. Whether you are serving to the forehand or backhand side, make sure your body is turned toward the spot on the front wall that you are aiming for. At the same time, take your racquet back as you would for your normal forehand. Then step toward the ball and in the direction of your target spot on the front wall. Make a full forward swing and stay as low as possible, below knee-level if possible, stroking through the ball and out toward the front wall. To guarantee power on the stroke, finish high.

Once you have served, move quickly into your ready position about two feet behind the short line in the center of the court.

THE LOB SERVE

The high-lob serve may not score outright service winners for you, as the drive serve can, but if hit correctly, it will force many weak returns from the receiver.

HIGH LOB SERVE

The high lob serve is hit high off the front wall and should strike the back sidewall deep, as shown in diagram, before bouncing. Photo shows ideal contact point for serving the high lob. Ball is met chest-high with an open racquet face. Stroke is forward and upward.

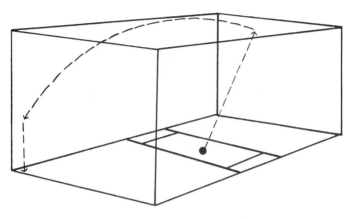

In the lob serve, you are concentrating on placement rather than pace. The idea is to hit the ball with a low-to-high stroking action so that it bounces off the front wall, then hits high on the left sidewall and drops deep in the left corner on your opponent's backhand side. If the ball hugs the sidewall on the way down, your opponent will not be able to return it aggressively. In the meantime, you'll have established good court position, with plenty of time to observe your opponent and anticipate the return.

If the high-lob serve is hit to the *forehand* side, the receiver may be able to move in and easily take it in the air. He can generate much more power on his return with his forehand, because his whole body is leaning into the shot. However, the occasional lob serve to the forehand is a good change of pace and keeps the opponent from getting too grooved in his return.

To hit the lob serve, stand sideways in the middle of the serving zone and pick as your target area on the front wall a spot about fifteen feet off the floor and 1–2 feet to the left of center. Let the ball bounce in front of you to a height of about three feet. Start your swing from a position below the apex of the bounce and hit up through the ball in a gentle, stroking motion. Finish high, then scamper into your ready position two feet behind the short line.

The lob serve must be hit much more softly

MEDIUM LOB SERVE

This serve is also called the garbage serve because it is hit with little power. The ball is played lower off the front wall than it is for the high lob, and should land just past the short line. Ideal contact point for the medium lob is slightly below waist level (see photo). Racquet slides slightly under the ball.

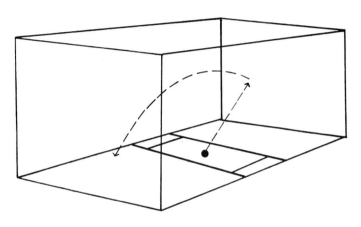

than the drive serve to achieve its objective. If it is hit with too much firmness, it will bounce off the back wall or sidewall with too much force and provide your opponent with a chance to play an aggressive return.

THE GARBAGE SERVE

The garbage serve is a lob serve that doesn't go as high or as far. The stroke is basically the same as the one used in making the lob, only the ball is played off the front wall about 8–10 feet from the floor, rather than the fifteen feet for the regular lob.

The goal is to hit the ball so softly that it just goes over the service line, without hitting the sidewall, and bounces low. This serve invites mistakes by the opponent. It appears so easy to return that the receiver often tries to do too much with it and ends up doing nothing. In making a mad rush for the ball, he may either hit the ball into the floor, or hit it so hard that it bounces off the back wall so far that the server has an easy set-up for his second shot.

The disadvantage of the garbage serve is that a smart opponent will take the ball out of the air—before the serve has had a chance to bounce—and hit it sharply crosscourt. His shot will be very hard to return if hit properly.

THE Z-SERVE, OR GARFINKEL SERVE

The Z-serve, or two-wall serve, is hit as hard as the drive, only it is aimed so that it travels on a diagonal or Z-shaped pattern and hits the front wall and a sidewall before shooting into the backcourt.

In 1971 the two serves that were being used almost exclusively were the high-lob serve and the medium-lob serve (garbage serve). About two months before the National Championships, I started experimenting with some different types of serves. I noticed that one serve took some weird bounces off the sidewall if I hit it correctly. This was the serve we know today as the Z-serve, hit with medium speed. I experimented with it in a few tournaments but didn't really use it that much.

In April 1971 the National Championships were held. In the second round, I had to play Charlie Brumfield, who was ranked number two in the world. Charles was giving me an artistic pasting. He had won the first game, 21–11, and was leading, 13–4, in the second game. I had tried everything to get back into the game except the serve that I had been practicing.

I switched to the medium Z-serve and it turned the match around. Brumfield had so much trouble returning the serve because of the unusual bounce that I won a great many easy points. I eventually

Z-SERVE

For this serve, whether the server plans to attack a right-handed opponent's forehand (diagram on left) or his backhand (diagram on right), the server stands about two feet away from the center of the service box in order to produce a sharply angled shot. Goal is to make the ball hit the front wall and sidewall quickly in succession so that shot flies directly into the opposite corner in the backcourt. Photo shows server at impact of Z-serve to opponent's backhand.

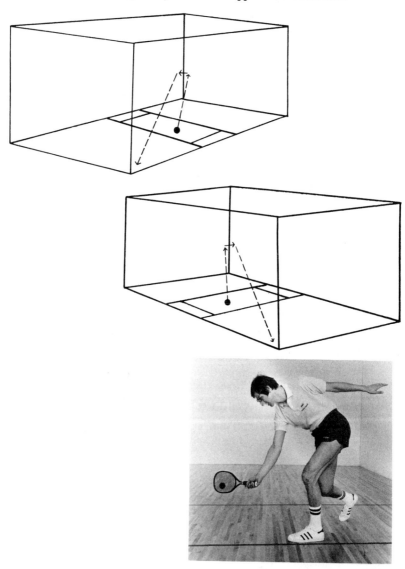

won the match, in what was to rank as one of my most satisfying victories in racquetball.

From that time on my friends and fans called this new Z-serve the "Garfinkel Serve."

To hit the Z-serve, you should take up a position a foot or two to the left or right of center in the serving zone. This gives you the proper angle for causing the ball to hit front wall and sidewall in quick succession before flying diagonally into the backcourt area. If you stand left of center, aim to hit the ball about 3–4 feet high on the front wall and about one foot from the right sidewall. If you stand right of center, aim at a spot one foot from the left sidewall.

If you stand in the left side of the serving zone, the Z-serve will finish in the left corner of the backcourt. If you stand in the right side, it will finish in the right corner.

The ideal Z-serve will hit the front wall, then the side wall and will bounce on the floor deep in the opposite corner just before striking the other sidewall, and then will bounce straight across the back wall. If hit perfectly, it will stay so close to the back wall that your opponent will be unable to get his racquet between the ball and the back wall.

To confuse your opponent, you can vary the speed of your Z-serve. To hit the Z-serve more slowly, you start in the same position as indicated above, but you aim at about 5–6 feet from the floor on the front wall. You can also experiment by moving closer or farther away from the center on the serve. However, don't forget the importance of establishing good court position *after* you serve.

SERVING STRATEGY

You can't expect to place your serves so well or hit them so hard that your opponent will never be able to return them. At the same time, you should not get into the habit of giving your opponent easy serves to handle. I recommend the following basic tactics on serving.

Since you have two serves to put the ball in play, make your first serve one of the more difficult serves we have discussed—the drive serve or the Z-serve. Use a lob serve or garbage serve and occasionally a slow Z-serve if you have to play a second serve, in order to get the ball in play and keep from doublefaulting.

Whether playing first or second serve, always take plenty of time in getting into position in the service box. Visualize where you're going to hit the ball off the front wall, and think about how hard you want to stroke it.

Use the type of serve that is most likely to force errors or weak returns from your opponent. Every racquetball player has strengths and weaknesses. Serve to your opponent's weaknesses most of the time. Mix up your serves by hitting to his strength now and then to keep him honest. Don't stick to the same serve, even if it is your favorite serve, if the opponent is able to handle it easily.

Here's a summary of the main points to remember when serving:

1. Take your time getting into position to serve in the box.

2. Prior to serving, turn around and check the receiver's position in the backcourt.

3. Use a wide variety of serves to keep your opponent off balance, but principally concentrate on attacking his weaknesses.

4. Use the forehand grip and stance.

5. Step toward the spot on the front wall that you intend to hit.

6. When making the drive serve or hard Z-serve, stay low, take a full swing, and follow through high. (Your body will partially hide the ball, making it a bit harder for your opponent to follow its path!)

7. When hitting the slower Z-serve, high-lob serve, or garbage serve, be sure to hit the ball softly enough so that it stays off the back wall.

8. Be sure to practice your serves during any warm-up before a match. Slow down or speed up serves according to the liveliness of the particular balls you are using.

Returning Serve

RACQUETBALL PLAYERS WHO FAIL TO DEVELOP A way to return serve effectively are in for a lot of frustration. Against a good server, they'll lose points outright on the return, or they'll produce such a weak return that the server has an easy set-up for his second shot.

Players who do learn a variety of effective service returns, on the other hand, often have the edge in matches with players of otherwise equal ability. So it's well worth taking the time to work on your own returns.

The serve itself dictates the type of return you, as the receiver, should try. In all cases, though, your goal is the same—to create a shot that forces the server to move out of the front court, not just to keep the ball in play.

Awaiting the serve, you should stand in the middle of the court, about 3–4 feet from the back wall. Make sure you're in a good ready position— prepared to change your grip, if necessary, and to move quickly to either side. Slight variations in this position are desirable in certain situations.

If you are playing an opponent who constantly hits hard drive-serves that land just over the short line, you should move up one more foot so you will be closer to the serve when he hits it.

You may also stand one foot to the right or left of center court if the server continually serves to the same side of the court. For example, if every serve is going to your backhand, you could move over one foot in that direction to be better prepared for the serve.

DRIVE SERVE—CEILING-BALL RETURN

As stated in the previous chapter, the drive serve is the most popular serve used in racquetball today. What can you do to return this serve effectively?

The *ceiling ball* is the best shot to try. For this shot, you want to play the ball to hit a spot on the ceiling 3–5 feet from the front wall and as close to the right or left sidewall as you can. If hit correctly, the ball will rebound off the front wall, bounce very high, and so force the server into the back of the court. This will give you an opportunity to move to

73

CEILING BALL RETURN

When playing good servers in racquetball, the percentage shot on return of serve is the ceiling ball, as shown in diagram. No effort is made to hit an aggressive shot because the server has forced the receiver into the deep corner on his weaker (backhand) side. Goal is to keep ball in play by lofting shot that hits the ceiling just before it strikes front wall. This should produce a return deep in the backcourt, forcing server away from center. Racquet is open at contact and stroke is slightly under the ball.

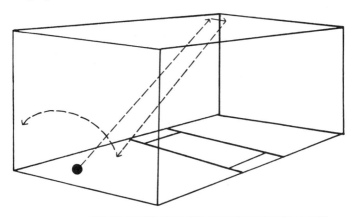

the center position in front court and take control of the action.

Once you see that the serve is going to be a hard-hit drive, move quickly to the side that the ball is coming to. Make sure that you take your racquet back as you move. Keep your eyes on the ball at all times. Turned sideways to the shot, drop your racquet low and meet the ball in front of you. Stay under the ball, continuing your swing upward and forward toward your target area on the ceiling.

You may find that your ceiling-ball return is bouncing off the back wall or sidewall and giving the server an easy ball to hit. If this happens, adjust your aim so that you're hitting a foot or two farther back on the ceiling.

DRIVE SERVE—CROSSCOURT RETURN

A hard crosscourt return can also be very effective against the drive serve, because it forces the server to retreat to the back of the court.

To make the crosscourt return, aim for a spot on the front wall about 2–4 feet high, about a foot to the right of center if you're on the left side of the court, and a foot to the left of center if you're returning from the right side.

As the ball approaches, get down as low as you can. Use the power of the oncoming serve to hit the shot sharply past the server. Remember to watch the ball, stand sideways, meet the ball in front of your body, and follow through high.

Z-SERVE—CEILING-BALL RETURN

Because the Z-serve can produce many unusual bounces, and because it sometimes hugs the sidewall, the only reasonably effective defense against it is the ceiling ball.

There is one major difference between this ceiling-ball return and the ceiling-ball return of the drive serve. The Z-serve usually comes off the sidewall in the back of the court, so it is vital that you don't crowd your swing. Make sure that you move far enough away from the sidewall so that you have room to maneuver. Many beginners panic when they see a Z-serve, get stuck next to the ball, and have no room at all to swing.

HIGH-LOB SERVE—CEILING-BALL OR
Z-BALL RETURN

A serve that is hit high and softly invites players to rush in and hit the ball as hard as they can—which often results in errors. So the high lob is one serve that must be returned carefully, whether you're hitting it with a little or a lot of power.

The safest way to return a high lob is with a

OTHER COMMON RETURNS

Diagrams show other returns that are possible, especially if serve is a weak one.

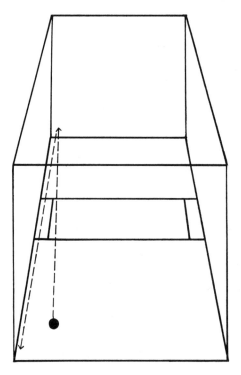

DRIVE RETURN. *Ball is played down the line and hard enough to force server to retreat to deep corner.*

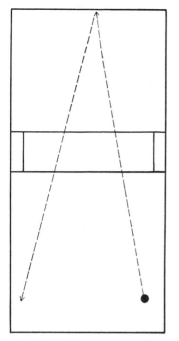

CROSSCOURT RETURN. *This shot must be played hard in order to pass the server on the rebound from the front wall.*

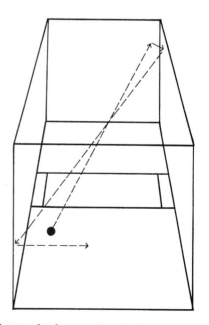

Z-BALL RETURN. *Shot is hit high into the front wall and close to sidewall. It produces an unusual bounce off sidewall, as shown, which will be hard for server to handle smoothly.*

ceiling ball. But a Z-ball return can also be effective, and makes a good change of pace. To play this shot, you should move in quickly in order to take the serve in the air. Hit the ball crosscourt to a spot on the front wall three feet below the ceiling.

The ball will rebound high off the front wall, hit high on the sidewall, then bounce crosscourt to the sidewall. It will hit the sidewall and shoot straight across the back of the court. If hit perfectly, the server will not be able to get his racquet between the ball and the back wall.

MEDIUM-LOB SERVE—CROSSCOURT RETURN

This is another serve that looks very easy to return—and is, provided you're careful not to rush in and hit it for all you're worth. Because of its slow bounce, you do have plenty of time to return the serve hard and accurately crosscourt. If you can take the serve in the air—before the ball bounces—you may be able to hit your return past the startled server before he has a chance to get set.

MEDIUM-LOB SERVE—DRIVE RETURN

The medium-lob serve can also be attacked with a low return. The ball should be hit in the air straight down the line, back in the same direction as it came from. If hit hard enough, it will get by the server before he has a chance to react. Your aiming point for this return should be no higher than 3–4 feet on the front wall.

IMPROVING SERVICE RETURNS

A good drill to improve service returns is to have a pro or helper expose you to all the different serves. Concentrate on returning the serves in such a way that the other player does not get an easy shot to hit. Remember, you are better off playing conservatively in returning serve. Your main goal is to get the server out of the front court.

SUMMARY OF RETURN OF SERVICE

1. Be in the proper ready position.
2. Move to the side where the ball is going.
3. Be prepared to switch your grip to the forehand or backhand, depending on which side the ball has been served to.
4. If you are returning a drive serve, the best return is to hit the ball to the ceiling.
5. Use the hard crosscourt return off the drive serve as a change of pace.
6. When returning the Z-serve, keep the ball

on the ceiling as much as possible.

7. When returning the high- or medium-lob serves, try to take them out of the air when possible.

8. Hit ceiling-, Z-, and hard-crosscourt returns off slower serves.

9. Don't give your opponent an easy service return to hit if at all possible.

Rallying

A *rally* REFERS TO ANY EXCHANGE OF SHOTS after the ball has been put into play. It is not to be confused with a *volley,* which is a shot played while the ball is still in the air (before it is allowed to bounce).

Many of the shots described as service returns may also be effectively employed during rallies. Ceiling balls are the most common shots seen during rallies. Many shots are hit to the ceiling, with other shots mixed in occasionally. Each player is waiting for an opportunity to produce one of the more aggressive shots described below.

OFFENSIVE SHOTS IN A RALLY

Diagrams show the most common point-winning shots played during rallys.

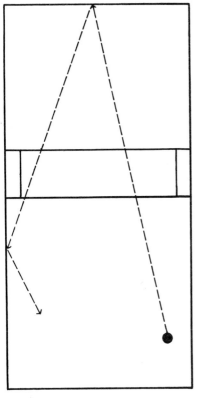

PASSING SHOT. *This is similar to the crosscourt service return except, for maximum effectiveness, the ball should hit sidewall after rebounding off front wall. If ball ricochets to back wall after hitting sidewall, it will be easier for opponent to retrieve.*

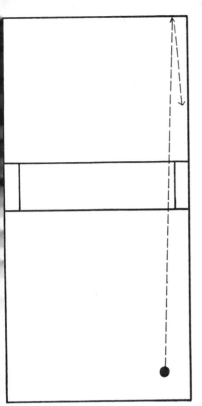

KILL SHOT. *The kill shot is hit as low as possible on the front wall, so that when it comes off the wall it is too low to the floor for opponent to play.*

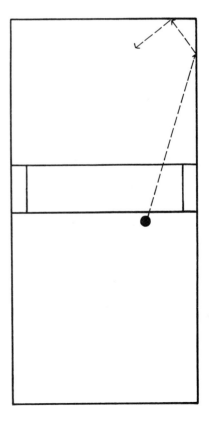

SIDEWALL OR PINCH SHOT. *This shot should not be tried unless you are in front of your opponent in the court. Try to hit the ball as low on the sidewall and as close to the front wall as possible. This will make the ball roll off low, as it does on the kill shot.*

THE KILL SHOT

The kill shot and the sidewall shot are the most aggressive shots in rallying and are best attempted when you have the serve. As the server, you can gamble more than the receiver, because if you miss a shot, you will only lose your serve. If the receiver misses a shot, he will lose the point.

Let's say you have served the ball and the receiver has given you a shot that has hit the front wall, bounced, and rebounded to the back wall. To make a kill shot, move quickly to the backcourt area so that you are in a good hitting-position as the ball comes off the back wall. If it is to the right side, you will be hitting a forehand. If it is to the left side, you will be hitting a backhand.

Try to hit the ball as hard as you can off the front wall. Hit down the line rather than crosscourt. The closer you hit the ball along the sidewall, the better. If the shot is on your forehand side, make sure that you have the forehand grip. Hold your racquet high. As you start your swing, make sure that your knees are slightly bent. As your racquet comes down into the ball, you should be bending lower and lower. You should be making contact well below knee-level. Swing through and follow-through high.

It is always better to hit your kill shots along

the sidewalls. Even if you do not roll the ball out flat it will still be very hard for your opponent to get his racquet between the ball and the sidewall to make the return. A kill shot hit crosscourt can be risky, because if your opponent is in front of you and you hit the ball too high off the front wall, he will have an easy set-up to return.

The kill shot may also be used against balls weakly played off the sidewall or front wall. Whether the opportunity to kill the ball occurs up close to the front wall, off the sidewall, or off the back wall, the basic stroke is the same.

THE SIDEWALL OR PINCH SHOT

If you're serving well, you will get many opportunities to hit sidewall shots. The best time to play this shot is when you get a weak service-return in the front court. In this situation, you're in front of your opponent and so blocking his view of the play. If you produce a shot that hits the sidewall first, the receiver will have great difficulty picking up the direction of the shot in time to do anything about it.

To hit this shot correctly, the ball should be aimed as close as possible to the front-wall/sidewall corner. The closer to the front wall that the shot hits on the sidewall, the better your sidewall shot will be. It will "pinch" near the crack in the corner and rebound at a short, sharp angle.

87

Whether on your *forehand* or *backhand,* you should start your swing as you would in the regular kill shot. Your body should be facing toward the sidewall near the front wall. Let the ball drop as low as possible, bring your racquet forward, and hit the ball when it is well below knee-level. Continue your forward swing and follow through high. If you hit the sidewall farther back, the ball will hit more toward the middle of the front wall, giving your opponent a better opportunity to make his return shot.

The sidewall shot may be used any time during a rally when you find yourself in front of your opponent with a short ball in the service-zone area. It's risky to try if your opponent is in front of you, because if the shot doesn't hit extremely low on the front wall after hitting the sidewall, your opponent will have a chance to kill the ball himself.

THE VOLLEY

To *volley* means to hit the ball in the air without letting it bounce. When you volley, you are trying to put the ball away or pass your opponent as quickly as possible. It requires much less of a backswing than other shots. Rather than taking a full swing at the ball, you hit it with a short, punching motion. You should make contact in front of you, swing straight through, and finish with a short follow-through.

SPECIALTY SHOTS

Varying court positions during a rally, and an assortment of unusual bounces, give advanced players a choice of shots to play. Some of the most effective ones are shown here.

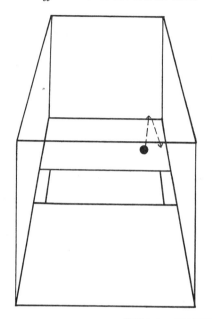

DROP SHOT. *Player must be well into front court to play this shot successfully. Idea is to stroke ball gently enough so that it comes off front wall and dies.*

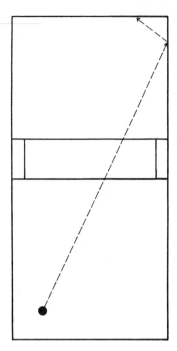

OVERHEAD. *This is an aggressive shot played to take advantage of a high-bouncing ball. Weight is forward to ensure power and control. Ball should be smashed low on the sidewall and as close to the front wall as possible.*

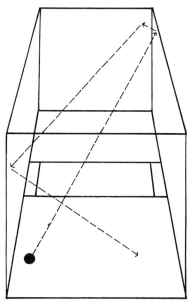

AROUND-THE-WALL BALL. *This shot is sometimes used as an alternative to a ceiling ball or Z-ball. Racquet is held at an angle and in front of body at impact to achieve desired trajectory.*

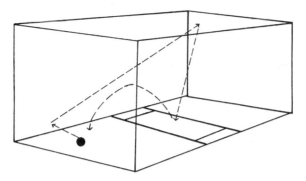

INTO-THE-BACK-WALL SHOT. *This is a desperation shot, to be tried only when you are well out of position and have no other choice. Ball must be hit forcefully off the back wall about five feet high to make it ricochet to the front wall in the air.*

If the server is hitting good serves, he will get some chances to take the receiver's weak return out of the air and volley it forcefully. This shot should be hit low, down the line rather than crosscourt, and as close to the sidewall as possible.

If the server is hitting weak serves, the receiver may be able to move in and volley the ball sharply crosscourt to get the server out of the serving area.

There are other times when you may want to volley a shot. During a rally, your opponent may be caught out of position in the backcourt. He will lazily float a shot to the front wall. Instead of letting the ball bounce, you should move up and hit the ball as hard and low as you can, straight and low off the front wall, close to the sidewall.

Volleying well will help you control the vital center-court position and will keep your opponent on the run behind you. You can actually wear an opponent down by volleying several balls away from him during a long rally.

DROP SHOTS

The drop shot should only be attempted when you are in the front court and your opponent is behind you. The idea is to hit the ball so gently that it dies when it hits the front wall and rebounds low to the floor. It's a risky touch-shot which incorrectly played gives the opponent an easy set-up for his next shot.

A good time to try the drop shot is when your serve has forced a weak return. If your opponent is deep in the backcourt with little chance to recover, you may score an outright winner.

Another time to try it, is when in a rally you have forced your opponent to hit you an easy shot from the backcourt. If you're in front of the short line, let the ball bounce and hit the drop shot.

The key to the shot is deception. After the ball has bounced off the front wall, start your swing as if you were about to hit a hard forehand or backhand kill-shot. Then suddenly slow your swing and gently push the ball to the front wall, as close as possible to the sidewall.

THE OVERHEAD SHOT

During some rallies, you may find that you and your opponent are trading ceiling balls. One way to change that pattern is by producing a Z-ball, as described on page 77. Another alternative is the overhead shot.

For the overhead, you must hit down on the ball very hard. This causes the shot to travel very fast off the low front wall. Even if your opponent is able to return the shot, he may give you an easy ball to hit on your next shot.

The disadvantage of the overhead is that it is an easy shot to hit into the floor. Or you may hit the sidewall or back wall in such a way that it results in giving your opponent a set-up.

You hit the overhead with a forehand grip. In preparing for the shot, take your racquet back, in the forehand grip, as you would for the ceiling ball. In fact, your opponent should not be able to tell whether you are planning to hit a ceiling ball or an overhead shot at this point. Plan to meet the ball when it is in front of you. As you start your forward swing, move your right foot, rather than your left foot, slightly forward. This will add power to your hitting motion. Hit down and forward on the ball. Continue all the way through and finish about waist-high.

You may hit the overhead effectively either down the line or crosscourt. If you're going down the line, try to hit the front wall about three feet from the floor. Going crosscourt, aim at about one foot to the left or right of center and about three feet from the floor. The ideal overhead shot should bounce twice before it hits the back wall.

THE OVERHEAD KILL-SHOT

The overhead kill-shot is a more aggressive version of the basic overhead. You should try this shot mostly when you are serving, because of the risk involved.

The idea is to hit the ball to the sidewall as close as possible to the front wall and as low as you can without risking hitting the floor.

THE AROUND-THE-WALL BALL

Another shot that can be used to break up ceiling-ball rallies is the around-the-wall ball. This shot is usually hit with a backhand stroke, when the player is positioned 5–7 feet from the back wall. It moves the opponent into the deep right corner and allows you to get out of the deep left backcourt. It also gives you an excellent opportunity to move to the center of the court and establish good center-court position.

Aim for a spot on the sidewall that is three feet from the ceiling and three feet from the front wall. If you hit this spot with the correct force, the ball will hit a sidewall, then front wall, then rebound to the opposite sidewall, just past the short line. After hitting the second sidewall, the ball then shoots to the opposite corner in the back of the court, and dies before it actually reaches the back wall. If hit too forcefully, it will rebound off the back wall too much and give your opponent an easy set-up.

PASSING SHOTS

Passing shots during a rally are a little different from the ones used on the service return.

You may find that your opponent is completely controlling the front of the court during a rally: he keeps hitting the ball so hard that you can only return the ball meekly to the front wall. In this situation, you may be able to use the power of your opponent's stroke to pass him.

When you hit the passing shot, you may be anywhere from three to six feet behind your opponent. Depending on whether you are on the left or the right side, you would be aiming for a spot one foot to the left or right of the middle of the front wall and about three feet from the floor. The ball should bounce past your opponent without hitting the sidewall and head for the deep right or deep left corner. The ideal passing shot will bounce twice before hitting any wall.

You may also hit the crosscourt passing-shot by first hitting the front wall and then hitting the sidewall. The problem with this is that if the ball strikes the sidewall too close to your opponent, he will have time to back up and get the shot.

Another good passing-shot is to hit the ball straight down the line. This can be risky if your opponent is able to take the ball out of the air and volley the shot straight down into the front wall. But it is quite effective if during a rally, you have moved your opponent to one side of the court. By hitting straight down the line, you will get the ball past your opponent before he gets to the other side.

To hit this passing shot, take your normal backswing, then swing straight through, aiming for a spot three feet high on the front wall near the sidewall. The ball should hit the front wall, bounce, and travel to either deep corner, depending on the side you hit.

THE BACKWALL SHOT

This is a shot that should be used only as a last resort. It is called for if your opponent has hit a great passing shot during a rally, and you can barely get to the ball. Hit it into the back wall as hard as you can. This will send the ball to the front wall and so keep it in play, but usually it leaves your opponent with a very easy shot to play next.

SUMMARY OF RALLYING

1. If you know a good variety of shots and can execute them correctly, you will be able to take charge of most rallies.
2. If you can't execute every shot correctly, you should use those shots that you feel most confident and comfortable with.
3. Play most shots to your opponent's backhand (weaker) side.
4. Try to control the center of the court and remain in front of your opponent as much as possible.
5. Try harder shots, such as the kill shot and

sidewall shot, when you're serving. If you do miss the shot, you only lose your serve, not a point.

6. As receiver, play defensively until you get an opening that calls for an offensive shot. Then—put it away!

Winning Racquetball Tactics

Once you've learned the basic strokes in racquetball and have sampled the competitive format a few times, you're ready to turn your attention to ways of developing your match-winning skills to the maximum. To win matches, you'll not only need good strokes, but also proper physical and mental attributes. The winning racquetball player is a thinking player—someone who knows what he or she is going to do, and how to go about it.

GETTING READY FOR THE MATCH

Before you step on the court, make sure you have broken a sweat by doing some light jogging. Also perform some stretching exercises to loosen your-self up.

Once you're on the court, begin to practice the shots that you will use in the match. Warm up from both sides of the court to make sure both your fore-hand and backhand shots are ready. Practice all of the types of serves you plan on using.

Usually, players take no more than five minutes to practice shots before beginning the match. You should work as hard as you possibly can during this brief time.

HOW FITNESS WILL HELP YOU WIN

If you're in top physical shape, you will be able to defeat most of the players who are equal to you in ability but who lack your fitness. You also may de-feat some players who are better than you are, be-cause of your superior physical conditioning. You will be able to keep the ball in play for long periods of time without worrying about getting tired.

When you have to make sudden starts and turns, you won't have to worry about pulled or torn muscles.

If a match is close, the physically fit player will have the edge going into the stretch. He will have that extra reserve to use to keep going, while an op-ponent who isn't in quite so good shape will be left standing and shaking his head in amazement at your stamina and staying power.

KNOWING YOUR OPPONENT'S WEAKNESSES

If you know your opponent's weaknesses, you can capitalize on them to win points. Here are some of the common weaknesses among racquetball players and how to exploit them.

WEAK BACKHAND

Among beginners, the backhand is a very weak shot, but many intermediate and advanced players also have weak backhands. Usually, such players have very good forehands, and will do everything possible to take the shot on their forehand. Many times, they will take shots on their forehand that should be a backhand shot.

I have seen so many players try to keep the ball over to the backhand side of their opponents without much success. Their opponents always run around the shot to take the ball on their forehand.

The correct way to capitalize on this weakness is to hit two or three shots (preferably ceiling balls) to the deep right corner. You will be opening up the whole left side. Then hit the ball sharply crosscourt to your opponent's backhand. He will have a difficult shot to hit

You should also mix up your serves from side

to side, so your opponent won't feel that every serve is coming to his backhand.

WEAK SECOND SERVE

If your opponent's second serve is very weak, you should attack it aggressively. Forget about going to the ceiling. Hit the return-shot hard cross-court to move the server out of the service box, or hit a hard drive down the line occasionally. If you are given a really easy set-up, you even may want to try a kill shot. However, don't try too many of these, as you could easily make an error.

LACK OF STAMINA

If you are playing someone who is not in top physical shape, run him! When you get a shot to hit that you can easily kill—don't! Hit a sharp cross-court shot instead. Make sure your opponent has to run to the back of the court. When he returns the shot, hit another crosscourt shot. Soon he won't be returning the shots. His lack of stamina will make him very tired and will result in your getting many easy shots to hit and put away.

CANNOT KILL THE BALL

A player may be in great shape, but if he cannot kill, or put the ball away, he is not going to win too many matches. Against a player like this you must be patient. Sooner or later, he will give you a shot that you can put away. A tremendous amount of pressure is taken off you by his inability to hit the ball low for a point. You should get many opportunities to score points.

NOT ENOUGH POWER

Many times you will face players who have nice strokes but don't hit the ball with any power. You should try to hit the ball as hard as you can. You want the ball to travel so fast that even if your opponent gets his racquet on the ball, he will be giving you many easy set-ups to hit, because he can't handle the pace of the shot.

POOR SERVICE RETURN

If a player has difficulty hitting effective service returns, you should try to hit as many hard drive-serves and Z-serves as you can. The more power and the more weird bounces that the ineffective receiver has to cope with, the more errors he will make.

TOO MUCH POWER

There's nothing that a hard hitter likes better than to play someone who tries to hit the ball harder than he does. When playing this type of player, hit slow serves and stay to the ceiling as much as possible. He will become very frustrated and will probably make many unforced errors by mishitting the slower shots.

PLAYER WATCHING THE FRONT WALL ONLY

If you are playing someone who doesn't turn and watch what you are doing when you are behind him, you can score many points. Make sure that you hit a wide variety of shots. I have found that side-wall shots are especially effective, as the opponent can't react quickly enough to determine the angle of the ball. Well-placed crosscourt shots and drives down the line are also effective.

CONTROLLING THE CENTER COURT

Usually, the player who is in control of the center-court area will win the match. Center court is the area of the floor starting from the service line and extending backward about five feet behind the short line. By being in this position, you never really have to go too far for any shot. You are also in front of your opponent most of the time.

HOW TO PLAY THE FIRST GAME

You must be ready to play as hard as you can from the opening point. We will assume that you have your game plan ready. If you win the service too,

INCORRECT—WATCHING FRONT WALL ONLY

CORRECT—CHECKING OPPONENT PRIOR TO CONTACT

One of the keys to rallying well in racquetball is to observe your opponent whenever he is hitting his shot, as this will give you a good idea what type of shot he will play. Turn back to watch front wall just as the opponent is about to make contact with ball.

start serving and try to get as many points as you can. Usually, you will hit mostly drive serves and Z-serves on your first serve. However, there are certain opponents, such as power hitters, against whom it might be advisable to use a slower serve so that you don't give them any pace. Play as aggressively as you can when you are serving. Hit slower serves on the second serve.

When you are not receiving, you should play defensively until you are given a shot that you can hit offensively. When you get this shot, put the ball away.

If you can win the first game, you have put your opponent under tremendous pressure. He must win the second game.

HOW TO PLAY THE SECOND GAME

If you have won the first game, continue doing the same things that you did in the first game. Concentrate and put the balls away. However, be prepared to change your game plan if your opponent changes his.

If you have lost the first game, you must stop and think about what you feel you were doing wrong. You must make adjustments in your game.

HOW TO PLAY THE TIEBREAKER

If the first two games are split, you will have to play a tiebreaker. Because the tiebreaker is played to only 11 points, the serve is very important in this deciding game. When you come in to serve, you should use drive serves and Z-serves. If you can run up a good lead, it will be very hard for your opponent to catch up. You must still play aggressively on offense and safely on defense.

You cannot afford to make mistakes in the tiebreaker.

WHAT TO DO WHEN YOU ARE AHEAD

When you are ahead and winning easily, it is very tempting to try some different shots. Don't! Use the same shots that have been winning for you. If your opponent changes his hitting patterns and starts catching up, then you will then have to adjust your game. However, you should never change a winning game if you are far ahead.

WHAT TO DO IF YOU ARE BEHIND

If you are losing, you must change your game plan.

If you are being overpowered, slow down the game. If you are being given very easy, soft shots with no pace on the ball, speed up the game.

If your serves aren't working, try different types of serves. Don't start to take foolish, low-percentage shots, as you will probably lose much faster. The longer that the ball stays in play the more time you will have to do something with it.

Remember: always change a losing game.

USE YOUR BEST SHOTS

If you get a shot down the center of the court and you have a choice of taking it on your forehand or backhand, take the shot on your forehand. It is usually the shot that you will have more confidence in.

Hit the shots that you hit best. If you positively cannot hit a hard drive-serve or Z-serve, then don't use these serves. If your forehand sidewall is your best shot, use that shot whenever you get the opportunity to do so. Conversely, don't try to pass your opponent if that isn't a shot you have confidence in.

OTHER PLAYING SITUATIONS

PLAYING THE SHOOTER

There are some players who seem to roll out every shot—produce shots that hit low off the front wall and barely bounce at all, making them very difficult to return. Such players never seem to miss, so you must beat them to the shot. You must try to shoot for a winner at the earliest opportunity that you are given. If you can show your opponent that you can make some shots as well as he can, you could put some doubts about his shooting ability in his head.

PLAYING MR. PSYCHE-OUT

Some players will do almost anything to ruin your concentration—stall, wipe imaginary sweat from the court, keep talking throughout the match, etc.

My advice is to completely ignore such a player. Under his seemingly confident manner there must be a lot of self-doubt. If he were sure of his abilities, he wouldn't have to try all of these shenanigans. If you can demonstrate that his actions don't bother you, you'll win the match much more easily than if he had kept his mouth shut.

PLAYING THE CHEATER

It's no fun playing an opponent who takes shots on two bounces, blocks you out when you have a shot, and who constantly complains about every shot. My advice is simply not to play any more matches with this individual.

PLAYING MORE THAN ONE PERSON

Do you have a standing date every Wednesday and Friday at five o'clock with your best friend? Is he your only racquetball opponent? Such an arrangement may be convenient, but probably neither one of you will improve very much. Try to play as many different players as you can. That way you'll get to know different styles and shots. You'll soon enjoy the challenge of trying different strategies and shots against different opponents.

PLAYING THE BETTER PLAYER

If you are playing an opponent who is far superior to you, stay relaxed and don't rush your shots. Watch the ball and take a full stroke every time you hit a shot. Don't try to put the ball away with shots that you never use. Be patient—wait for the right opportunity to kill the ball. Usually, the player who is overmatched will try to put the ball away every time that he hits it, but this will only result in his losing much faster.

PLAYING THE LEFT-HANDER

Too many right-handers try to change tactics when playing a left-hander, but this usually confuses rather than helps them.

When playing a lefty, you should hit most of your serves to his backhand. You would also hit most of your ceiling balls to his backhand. However, when you have a shot that you can put away, hit it in the same spot you would if you were playing a right-hander.

For instance, if you have a set-up off the back

wall on your backhand, and that is one of your best shots, shoot the ball straight down the line, just as you would if you were playing a righty. If you hit the ball low enough, the lefty has no chance to return the ball, even if it is on his forehand.

WHEN SHOULD YOU PLAY YOUR HARDEST?

Certain players always seem to win the games that end by the scores of 21–18 or 21–19. Why? They seem to have that fierce desire to win no matter what they have to do. I don't mean that they will cheat. But they will go after every ball, no matter where it is on the court. They will make the shots that they know they have to make. They will summon that extra mental and physical strength that they need. They will not be beaten. You must play your hardest when you are close to victory, and even harder if you are close to defeat.

SUMMARY

1. Be in shape.
2. Have a game plan ready for your opponent.
3. Be ready to play as hard on the first point as on the last point of the match.
4. Attempt to get off to a fast start.

5. Stay with a winning game.
6. Change a losing game.
7. Use the shots that you can utilize best.
8. Attempt to control center-court position.
9. Watch your opponent as he begins his shot.
10. Concentrate by playing your hardest at all times.

Doubles

BEFORE YOU ATTEMPT TO PLAY DOUBLES, MAKE SURE you are reasonably skillful in singles. In singles, you only need to know where your opponent is. In doubles, you must know where your partner and the two players on the opposing team are at all times. Doing so will result in your having good court-position and being better prepared to hit your shots.

In playing doubles, there are a few basic rules that will help you greatly. They are:

1. Scoring is the same as in singles.
2. Be sure to give your opponents a clear view of the ball at all times.
3. Don't crowd your opponents when they are hitting the ball.

4. When your partner or either of your opponents is hitting the ball, try to watch him as he starts his swing. You will have a much better idea of where the ball is going.

5. Always encourage your partner.

6. Don't say, "I'm sorry"—your partner knows you didn't miss the ball on purpose.

7. Choose a partner who you enjoy playing with. This will make the game much more fun.

Doubles teams play either side-by-side or up-and-back in the court. The better formation for most situations is to play side-by-side, with each player taking responsibility for shots hit on his own side.

Imagine a line running down the middle of the court, dividing the court in half. Each shot on the right side of the imaginary line would be taken by the player who is playing to the right of the line. Each shot on the left side would be taken by the player who plays to the left of the line.

Which player should play which side? If one player is left-handed and his partner is right-handed, the choices are easy. The right-hander should play the right side and the left-hander should play the left side. In this way, any shots that are hit anywhere on the court, including hard down-the-line shots, could be taken on a forehand of the righty-lefty combination. A good righty-lefty team is hard to beat.

But most teams usually feature two right-handers. In these cases, the better backhand player should play the left side. He will be able to handle the shots that go to the backhand-side down the left sidewall. He would also take most of the shots that come down the middle of the court, as they are on his forehand. The right-side player would be able to handle most of the shots that are along the right sidewall.

When one player is much better than his partner, he should definitely play the left side. This is because most of the play in racquetball tends to go to that side. Each team strives to keep the ball in the deep left corner, and it takes good skill to shoot from that position.

GENERAL STRATEGY AND PLAY

Before you begin your doubles match, you and your partner should decide who is going to serve first, who will take shots that are down the middle, and the types of shots that will help you win against the team you are playing. By settling all this beforehand, both of you will be much better prepared mentally to play the match. You will find yourself in the correct position most of the time, instead of running all over the court not knowing exactly what your role is.

The team that wins the toss should elect to serve first and so get some points on the board. The first

CORRECT STARTING POSITION IN DOUBLES. *Serving team stands in the service zone, with server preparing to serve and server's partner remaining in doubles service box until serve is made. Opposing team is in backcourt ready to return the serve.*

server up continues serving until his side loses serve. Next time his side regains the serve, he and his partner alternate on serve until the side loses serve.

The server's partner must stand in one of the two small boxes between the service and short lines. He cannot move past the short line until the ball has passed the short line in the air. He is better off standing in the box on the side that he plays. In that way, he can move straight back a foot or two into position.

In doubles, you should constantly be hitting drive serves and Z-serves. Since there are four players on the court, the receiving team's area in which to return the ball is much smaller than in singles. If they have to hit a ball that is coming very fast or is bouncing crazily off the sidewalls or back wall, they can become very frustrated.

You should try to keep all serves out of the middle of the court. They should be hit deep into the far corners in the back of the court. You can also serve the Z-serves so that they hit deep off the back sidewalls. You can also try serving just over the short line, but this is a risky serve if it is not hit just right.

On the second serve, it is better to hit medium or slow Z-serves than lobs. You will still be forcing the receiving team to hit a good service return. Be careful that you do not double-fault.

The serving team tries to control the center of the court, as in singles. Always try to stay in front of your opponents. If you are serving well, the receiving team will always be scrambling from a defensive position, as you will have the center blocked. In doubles, the weaker player can sometimes be played to at will. The serving team can hit all of its serves and shots to the weaker player and thus practically keep his partner out of the play altogether.

The serving team should think strictly offensively, using as many kill shots, sidewall pinchshots, and passing shots as possible. Only if the servers are in trouble should they go to the ceiling ball or Z-ball. Drop shots and volleys can be especially effective if both opponents are in deep backcourt and you are far up in the front court.

When either partner on the serving team is hitting a shot from backcourt, his partner should move up toward the front court on his own side. If his partner's shot is returned, he will be better able to return a shot that is hit in the area from the short line to the front wall.

There will be other times when you wind up on your partner's side of the court because of a mixup in positioning. Do not panic. Make your shot and then switch back to your normal side.

THE RECEIVING TEAM

Both players on the receiving team should have their game plan formulated as to return of serve. They should have patience and play defensively until they get an opportunity to put the ball away or pass their opponents.

When receiving serve, both left-court and right-court players should be about 3–4 feet from the back wall and about five feet from the sidewall.

When returning serve in doubles, you should try everything in your power to return the ball to the ceiling. You are trying to move the serving team out of center court and assume that position yourselves.

If you try to shoot the ball for a winner and hit it a shade too high off the front wall, you will be giving the serving team an easy set-up, as they are already in front court. If you try to pass and the ball is hit too high off the front wall, it will rebound off the back wall, giving the serving team an easy shot to hit.

You must try to hit the ceiling ball in such a way as to keep the shots off the back wall and sidewalls.

Try to keep in mind at all times when you are receiving serve and on defense, that if you win the rally, you get the server out of serve. If you lose the rally, you lose the point.

SUMMARY OF MAIN POINTS IN DOUBLES

1. Decide which players will play which side.
2. Have a game plan ready.

3. Concentrate very hard when you are serving.
4. Play offensively when serving.
5. Play defensively when returning serve.
6. On defense, don't shoot until you have a chance to do so.

OFFICIAL U.S.R.A. – N.R.C.
FOUR-WALL RULES

PART I – THE GAME

Rule 1.1 - Types of Games. Racquetball may be played by two or four players. When played by two it is called "singles;" and when played by four, "doubles."

Rule 1.2 - Description. Racquetball is a competitive game in which a racquet is used to serve and return a ball.

Rule 1.3 - Objective. The objective is to win each rally by serving or returning the ball so the opponent is unable to keep the ball in play. A rally is won when a side is unable to return the ball before it touches the floor twice.

Rule 1.4 - Points and Outs. Points are scored only by the serving side when it serves an ace or wins a rally. When the serving side loses a rally, it loses the serve. Losing the serve is called a "side-out" or "hand-out."

Rule 1.5 - Game. A game is won by the side first scoring 21 points.

Rule 1.6 - Match. A match is won by the side first winning two games.

Rule 1.7 - Tie-breaker. In the event each side wins a game, the third game will be won by the side first scoring 11 points. This 11 point third game is called "tie-breaker."

PART II. COURT AND EQUIPMENT

Rule 2.1 - Court. The specifications for a standard four-wall racquetball court are:

(a) Dimensions. The dimensions shall be 20 feet wide, 20 feet high and 40 feet long with each back wall at least 12 feet high.

(b) Lines and Zones. Racquetball courts shall be divided and marked on the floors with 1½ inch wide red or white lines as follows:

(1) Short Line. The short line divides the court in half, parallel to the front and back walls. The back edge of the short line shall be equal distance between the front and back walls, 20 feet from both.

(2) Service Line. The service line is parallel with the short line with the front edge of the service line five feet in front of the back edge of the short line.

(3) Service Zone. The service zone is the space between the outer edges of the short line.

(4) The service box lines are located at each end of the service zone and designated by lines 18 inches from and parallel with each side wall.

(5) Service Boxes. The service boxes are the spaces between the side walls and the service box lines.

(6) Receiving Lines. Five feet back of the short line, vertical lines shall be marked on each side wall extending 3 inches from the

floor. The back edges of the receiving lines shall be five feet from the back edge of the short line.

Rule 2.2 - Ball Specifications. The specification for the standard racquetball are:

(a) **Size:** The ball shall be 2¼ inches in diameter.
(b) **Weight:** The ball shall weigh approximately 1.4 ounces.
(c) **Bounce:** The ball shall bounce 68-72 inches from a 100 inch drop at a temperature of 76 degrees F.

(d) **Official Ball.** The official ball of the U.S.R.A. is the black Seamco 558; the official ball of the N.R.C. is the green Seamco 559; or any other racquetball deemed official by the U.S. R.A. or N.R.C. from time to time.

Rule 2.3 - Ball Selection. A ball shall be selected by the game referee for use in each match in all tournaments. During a game the referee may, at his discretion or at the request of both players or teams, select another ball. Balls that are not round or which bounce erratically shall not be used.

(a) In tournament play, the referees all choose at least two balls for use, so that in the event of breakage, the second ball can be put into play immediately.

Rule 2.4 - Racquet. The official racquet will have a maximum head length of 11 inches and a width of 9 inches. These measurements are computed from the outer edge of the racquet head rims. The handle may not exceed 7 inches in length. Total length and width of the racquet may not exceed a total of 27 inches.

(a) The racquet must include a thong which must be securely wrapped on the player's wrist.

(b) The racquet frame may be made of any material, as long as it conforms to the above specifications.

(c) The strings of the racquet may be gut, monofilament, nylon or metal.

Rule 2.5 - Uniform. All parts of the uniform, consisting of shirt, shorts and socks, shall be clean, white or of bright colors. Warm-up pants and shirts, if worn in actual match play, shall also be white or of bright colors, but may be of any color if not used in match play. Only club insignia, name of club, name of racquetball organization, name of tournament, or name of sponsor may be on the uniform. Players may not play without shirts.

PART III. OFFICIATING

Rule 3.1 — Tournaments. All tournaments shall be managed by a committee or chairman, who shall designate the officials.

Rule 3.2 - Officials. The officials shall include: (a) A referee for all matches. (b) A referee and two linesmen for all quarter-final, semi-final, championship and third place matches. (c) Additional officials, assistants, scorekeepers or record keepers may be designated as desired.

Rule 3.3 - Qualifications. All officials shall be experienced or trained, and shall be thoroughly familiar with these rules and with the local playing conditions.

Rule 3.4 - Briefing. Before each match the

officials and players shall be briefed on rules and on local court hinders or other regulations.

Rule 3.5 - Referees. (a) **Pre-Match Duties**. Before each match commences, it shall be the duty of the referee to:

(1) Check on adequacy of preparation of the court with respect to cleanliness, lighting and temperature.

(2) Check on availability and suitability of all materials necessary for the match such as balls, towels, score cards and pencils.

(3) Check readiness and qualifications of assisting officials.

(4) Explain court regulations to players and inspect the compliance of racquets with rules upon request.

(5) Remind players to have an adequate supply of extra racquets and uniforms.

(6) Introduce players, toss coin, and signal start of first game.

(b) **Decisions**. During games the referee shall decide all questions that may arise in accordance with these rules. In National events (i.e., pro tour, regionals, National Championships, National Juniors or any other event deemed "National" by the USRA or NRC, a protest shall be decided by the National Director, or in his absence the National Commissioner, or in his absence the National Coordinator, or any other person delegated by the National Director. On all questions involving judgment and on all questions not covered by these rules, the decision of the referee is final.

(c) Protests. Any decision not involving the judgment of the referee may on protest be decided by the chairman, if present, or his delegated representative.

(d) Forfeitures. A match may be forfeited by the referee when:

(1) Any player refuses to abide by the referee's decision, or engages in unsportsmanlike conduct.

(2) After warning, any player leaves the court without permission of the referee during a game.

(3) Any player for a singles match, or any team for a doubles match fails to report to play. Normally, 20 minutes from the scheduled game time will be allowed before forfeiture. The tournament chairman may permit a longer delay if circumstances warrant such a decision.

(4) If any player for a singles, or any team for a doubles fail to appear to play any matches or play-offs, they shall forfeit their ratings for future tournaments and forfeit any trophies, medals, awards òr prize money.

(e) "Referee's Technical." The referee is empowered, after giving due warning, to deduct one point from a contestant's or his team's total score when in the referee's sole judgment, the contestant during the course of the match is being overtly and deliberately abusive beyond a point of reason. The warning referred to will be called a "**Technical Warning**" and the actual invoking of this penalty is called a "**Referee's Technical.**" If after the technical is called against the abusing contestant and the play is not immediately continued within the alloted time provided for under the existing rules, the referee is empowered to forfeit the match in favor of the abusing contestant's opponent or opponents as the case may be. The **"Referee's Technical"** can be invoked by the referee as many times during the course of a match as he deems necessary.

(f) **Profanity**. No warning need be given by the referee, and an immediate "Referee's Technical" may be invoked by the referee if a player utters profane language in any way.

Rule 3.6 - Scorers. The scorer may keep a record of the progress of the game in the manner prescribed by the committee or chairman. As a minimum the progress record shall include the order of serves, timeouts, and points. The referee may at his discretion also serve as scorer.

Rule 3.7 - Record Keepers. In addition to the scorer, the committee may designate additional persons to keep more detailed records for statistical purposes of the progress of the game.

Rule 3.8 - Linesmen. Two linesmen will be designated by the tournament chairman or referee and shall, at the referee's signal, either agree or disagree with the referee's ruling.

The official signal by a linesman to show agreement with the referee is "thumbs up." The official signal to show disagreement is "thumbs down." The official signal for no opinion is an "open palm down."

If both linesmen disagree with the referee, the referee must reverse his ruling. If one linesman agrees and one linesman disagrees or has no

opinion the referee's call shall stand. If one linesman disagrees and one linesman has no opinion,
the rally shall be re-played.

Rule 3.9 - Appeals. In any match using linesmen, a player or team may appeal certain calls by
the referee. These calls are 1) kill shots (whether
good or bad); 2) fault serves; and 3) double
bounce pick ups. At no time may a player or
team appeal hinder, avoidable hinder or technical
foul calls.

The appeal must be directed to the referee,
who will then request opinions from the linesmen.
Any appeal made directly to a linesman by a
player or team will be considered null and void,
and forfeit any appeal rights for that player or
for that particular rally.

(a) **Kill-Shot Appeals.** If the referee makes
a call of "good" on a kill shot attempt which ends
a particular rally, the loser of the rally may appeal
the call, if he feels the shot was not good. If the
appeal is successful and the referee's original call
reversed, the player who originally lost the rally
is declared winner of the rally and is entitled to
every benefit under the rules, i.e., point and/or
service.

If the referee makes a call of "bad" of "skip"
on a kill shot attempt, he has ended the rally. The
player against whom the call went has the right
to appeal the call, if he feels the shot was good. If
the appeal is successful and the referee's original
call reversed, the player who originally lost the
rally is declared winner of the rally and is entitled
to every benefit under the rules as winner of a
rally.

(b) **Fault Serve Appeals.** If the referee makes a call of "fault" on a serve that the server felt was good, the server may appeal the call. If his appeal is successful, the server is then entitled to two additional serves.

If the served ball was considered by the referee to be an ace and in his opinion there was absolutely no way for the receiver to return the serve, then a point shall be awarded to the server.

If the referee makes a "no call" on a particular serve (therefore making it a legal serve) but either player feels the serve was short, either player may appeal the call at the end of the rally. If the loser of the rally appeals and wins his appeal, then the situation reverts back to the point of service with the call becoming fault. If it was a first service, one more serve attempt is allowed. If the server already had one fault, the second fault would cause a side out.

(c) **Double bounce pick-up appeals.** If the referee makes a call of "two bounces," thereby stopping play, the player against whom the call was made has the right of appeal, if he feels he retrieved the ball legally. If the appeal is upheld, the rally is re-played.

If the referee makes no call on a particular play during the course of a rally in which one player feels his opponent retrieved a ball on two or more bounces, the player feeling this way has the right of appeal. However, since the ball is in play, the player wishing to appeal must clearly motion the referee and linesmen by raising his non-racquet hand, thereby alerting them to the exact play which is being appealed. At the same time, the player appealing must continue to retrieve and play the rally.

If the appealing player should win the rally, no appeal is necessary. If he loses the rally, and his appeal is upheld, the call is reversed and the "good" retrieve by his opponent becomes a "double bounce pick-up," making the appealing player the winner of the rally and entitled to all benefits thereof.

Rule 3.10 - If at any time during the course of a match the referee is of the opinion that a player or team is deliberately abusing the right of appeal, by either repetitious appeals of obvious rulings, or as a means of unsportsmanlike conduct, the referee shall enforce the Technical Foul rule.

PART IV. PLAY REGULATIONS

Rule 4.1 - **Serve-Generally.** (a) **Order.** The player or side winning the toss becomes the first server and starts the first game. The loser of the toss will serve first in the second game. The player or team scoring more points in games one and two combined shall serve first in the tie-breaker. In the event that both players or teams score an equal number of points in the first two games, another coin toss shall be held prior to the tie-breaker with the winner of the toss serving first.

(b) **Start.** Games are started from any place within the service zone. No part of either foot may extend beyond either line of the service zone. Stepping on the line (but not beyond it) is permitted. Server must remain in the service zone until the served ball passes the short line. Violations are called "foot faults."

(c) **Manner.** A serve is commenced by bouncing the ball to the floor in the service zone, and on the first bounce the ball is struck by the server's racquet so that it hits the front wall and on the rebound hits the floor back of the short line, either with or without touching one of the side walls.

(d) Readiness. Serves shall not be made until the receiving side is ready, or the referee has called play ball.

(e) Deliberate Delays. Deliberate delays on the part of the server or receiver exceeding 10 seconds shall result in an out or point against the offender.

(1) This "10 second rule" is applicable to both server and receiver, each of whom is allowed up to 10 seconds to serve or be ready to receive. It is the server's responsibility to look and be certain the receiver is ready. If the receiver is not ready, he must signal so by raising his racquet above his head. Such raising of the racquet is the only legal signal that the receiver may make to alert the referee and server that he is not ready.

(2) If the server serves a ball while the receiver is signaling "not ready" the serve shall go over with no penalty.

(3) If the server looks at the receiver and the receiver is not signalling "not readiness" the server may then serve. If the receiver attempts to signal "not ready" after this point such signal shall not be acknowledged and the serve becomes legal.

(f) Time Outs. At no time shall a call of "time out" by a player be acknowledged by the referee if the "time out" call does not precede the serve, i.e., the so-called "Chabot time-out," is not legal. The beginning of the serve, as indicated in rule 4.1 C, is with the bounce of the ball.

Rule 4.2 - Serve - In Doubles. (a) Server. At the beginning of each game in doubles, each side shall inform the referee of the order of service which order shall be followed throughout the game. Only the first server serves the first time up and continues to serve first throughout the game. When the first server is out—the side is out. Thereafter both players on each side shall serve until a hand-out occurs. It is not necessary for the server to alternate serves to their opponents.

(b) Partner's Position. On each serve, the server's partner shall stand erect with his back to the side wall and with both feet on the floor within the service box until the served ball passes the short line. Violations are called "foot faults" subject to penalties thereof.

Rule 4.3 - Defective Serves. Defective serves are of three types resulting in penalties as follows:

(a) Dead Ball Serve. A dead ball serve results in no penalty and the server is given another serve without cancelling a prior illegal serve.

(b) Fault Serve. Two fault serves result in a hand-out.

(c) Out Serves. An out serve results in a hand-out.

Rule 4.4 - Dead Ball Serves. Dead ball serves do not cancel any previous illegal serve. They occur when an otherwise legal serve:

(a) Hits Partner. Hits the server's partner on the fly on the rebound from the front wall while the server's partner is in the service box. Any serve that touches the floor before hitting the partner in the box is a short.

(b) **Screen Balls**. Passes too close to the server or the server's partner to obstruct the view of the returning side. Any serve passing behind the server's partner and the side wall is an automatic screen.

(c) **Court Hinders**. Hits any part of the court that under local rules is a dead ball.

Rule 4.5 - **Fault Serves**. The following serves are faults and any two in succession results in a handout:

(a) **Foot Faults**. A foot fault results:

(1) When the server leaves the service zone before the served ball passes the short line.

(2) When the server's partner leaves the service box before the served ball passes the short line.

(b) **Short Service**. A short service is any served ball that first hits the front wall and on the rebound hits the floor in front of the back edge of the short line either with or without touching one side wall.

(c) **Three-Wall Serve**. A three-wall serve is any ball served that first hits the front wall and on the rebound hits two side walls on the fly.

(d) **Ceiling Serve**. A ceiling serve is any served ball that touches the ceiling after hitting the front wall either with or without touching one side wall.

(e) **Long Serve**. A long serve is any served ball that first hits the front wall and rebounds to the back wall before touching the floor.

(f) **Out of Court Serve.** Any ball going out of the court on the serve.

Rule 4.6 - Out Serves. Any one of the following serves results in a handout:

(a) A serve in which the ball is struck after being bounced outside the service zone.

(b) **Missed Ball.** Any attempt to strike the ball on the first bounce that results either in a total miss or in touching any part of the server's body other than his racquet.

(c) **Non-front Serve.** Any served ball that strikes the server's partner, or the ceiling, floor or side wall, before striking the front wall.

(d) **Touched Serve.** Any served ball that on the rebound from the front wall touches the server or touches the server's partner while any part of his body is out of the service box or the server's partner intentionally catches the served ball on the fly.

(e) **Out-of-Order Serve.** In doubles, when either partner serves out of order.

(f) **Crotch Serve.** If the served ball hits the crotch in the front wall it is considered the same as hitting the floor and is an out. A crotch serve into the back wall (or side wall on three wall serves) is good and in play.

Rule 4.7 - Return of Serve. (a) The receiver or receivers may not infringe on the "five foot zone" until the server strikes the ball. The receiver may then "rush" the serve and return it after the served ball passes the short line, as long as no part of the receiver's body or racquet breaks the plane of the service zone.

(b) **Defective Serve**. To eliminate any misunderstanding, the receiving side should not catch or touch a defectively served ball until called by the referee or it has touched the floor the second time.

(c) **Fly Return**. In making a fly return the receiver must end up with both feet back of the service zone. A violation by a receiver results in a point for the server.

(d) **Legal Return**. After the ball is legally served, one of the players on the receiving side must strike the ball with his racquet either on the fly or after the first bounce and before the ball touches the floor the second time to return the ball to the front wall either directly or after touching one or both side walls, the back wall or the ceiling, or any combination of those surfaces. A returned ball may not touch the floor before touching the front wall. (1) It is legal to return the ball by striking the ball into the back wall first, then hitting the front wall on the fly or after hitting the side wall or ceiling. (2) If the ball should strike the front wall, then back wall and then front wall again without striking the floor, the player whose turn it is to strike the ball, may do so by letting the ball bounce after hitting the front wall a second time. (3) If the ball strikes the front wall, then back wall, and then front wall again after striking the floor, the player whose turn it is to strike the ball must do so by striking it before it hits the floor a second time.

(e) **Failure to Return**. The failure to return a serve results in a point for the server.

Rule 4.8 - Changes of Serve. (a) Hand-out.
A server is entitled to continue serving until:

(1) **Out Serve.** He makes an out serve under Rule 4.6 or

(2) **Fault Serves.** He makes two fault serves in succession under Rule 4.5, or

(3) **Hits Partner.** He hits his partner with an attempted return, or

(4) **Return Failure.** He or his partner fails to keep the ball in play by returning it as required by Rule 4.7 (d), or

(5) **Avoidable Hinder.** He or his partner commits an avoidable hinder under Rule 4.11.

(b) **Side-out** (1) In Singles. In singles, retiring the server retires the side.

(2) In Doubles. In doubles, the side is retired when both partners have been put out, except on the first serve as provided in Rule 4.2 (a).

(c) Effect. When the server or the side loses the serve, the server or serving side shall become the receiver; and the receiver or receiving side, the server; and so alternately in all subsequent services of the game.

Rule 4.9 - Rallies. Each legal return after the serve is called a rally. Play during rallies shall be according to the following rules:

(a) **One or Both Hands.** Only the head of the racquet may be used at any time to return the ball. The ball must be hit with the racquet in one or both hands. Switching hands to hit a ball is an out. The use of any portion of the body is an out.

(b) **One Touch.** In attempting returns, the

138

ball may be touched only once by one player on returning side. In doubles both partners may swing at, but only one, may hit the ball. Each violation of (a) or (b) results in a handout or point.

(c) **Return Attempts.** (1) **In Singles.** In singles if a player swings at but misses the ball in play, the player may repeat his attempts to return the ball until it touches the floor the second time.

(2) **In Doubles.** In doubles if one player swings at but misses the ball, both he and his partner may make further attempts to return the ball until it touches the floor the second time. Both partners on a side are entitled to an attempt to return the ball.

(3) **Hinders.** In singles or doubles, if a player swings at but misses the ball in play and in his or his partner's attempt again to play the ball there is an unintentional interference by an opponent it shall be a hinder. (See Rule 4.10.)

(d) **Touching Ball.** Except as provided in Rule 4.10(a) (2), any touching of a ball before it touches the floor the second time by a player other than the one making a return is a point or out against the offending player.

(e) **Out of Court Ball.** (1) **After Return.** Any ball returned to the front wall which on the rebound or on the first bounce goes into the gallery or through any opening in a side wall shall be declared dead and the serve replayed.

(2) **No Return.** Any ball not returned to the front wall, but which caroms off a player's racquet into the gallery or into any opening in a side wall either with or without touch-

ing the ceiling, side or back wall, shall be an out or point against the player or players failing to make the return.

(f) **Dry Ball**. During the game and particularly on service every effort should be made to keep the ball dry. Deliberate wetting shall result in an out.

(g) **Broken Ball**. If there is any suspicion that the ball has broken during the serve, or during a rally, play shall continue until the end of the rally. The referee or any player may request the ball be examined. If the referee decides the ball is broken or otherwise defective, a new ball shall be put into play and the rally replayed.

(h) **Ball Inspection**. The ball may be inspected by the referee between rallies at any time during a match.

(i) **Play Stoppage**. (1) If a player loses a shoe or other equipment, or foreign objects enter the court, or any other outside interference occurs, the referee shall stop the play. (2) Players wearing protective eye glasses have the responsibility of having such eyeglasses securely fastened. In the event that such protective eye glasses should become unfastened and enter the court, the play shall be stopped as long as such eyeglasses were fastened initially. In the event such eye glasses are not securely fastened, no stoppage of play shall result and the player wearing such glasses plays at his own risk. (3) If a player loses control of his racquet, time should be called after the point has been decided, providing the racquet does not strike an opponent or interfere with ensuing play.

Rule 4.10 - Dead Ball Hinders. Hinders are

of two types — "dead ball" and "avoidable." Dead ball hinders as described in this rule result in the rally being replayed. Avoidable hinders are described in Rule 4.11.

(a) **Situations.** When called by the referee, the following are dead ball hinders:

(1) **Court Hinders.** Hits any part of the court which under local rules is a dead ball.

(2) **Hitting Opponent.** Any returned ball that touches an opponent on the fly before it returns to the front wall.

(3) **Body Contact.** Any body contact with an opponent that interferes with seeing or returning the ball.

(4) **Screen Ball.** Any ball rebounding from the front wall close to the body of a player on the side which just returned the ball to interfere with or prevent the returning side from seeing the ball. See Rule 4.4 (b).

(5) **Strattle Ball.** A ball passing between the legs of a player on the side which just returned the ball, if there is no fair chance to see or return the ball.

(6) **Back Swing Hinder.** If there is body contact on the back swing, the player must call it immediately. This is the only hinder call a player can make.

(7) **Other Interference.** Any other unintentional interference which prevents an opponent from having a fair chance to see or return the ball.

(b) **Effect.** A call by the referee of a "hinder" stops the play and voids any situation following such as the ball hitting a player. No player is authorized to call a hinder, except on the back swing and such a call must be made immediately, as provided in Rule 4.10 (a)(6).

(c) **Avoidance.** While making an attempt to return the ball, a player is entitled to a fair chance to see and return the ball. It is the duty of the side that has just served or returned the ball to move so that the receiving side may go straight to the ball and not be required to go around an opponent. The referee should be liberal in calling hinders to discourage any practice of playing the ball where an adversary cannot see it until too late. It is no excuse that the ball is "killed," unless in the opinion of the referee the ball couldn't be returned. Hinders should be called without a claim by a player, especially in close plays and on game points.

(d) **In Doubles.** In doubles, both players on a side are entitled to a fair and unobstructed chance at the ball and either one is entitled to a hinder even though naturally it would be his partner's ball and even though his partner may have attempted to play the ball or that he may already have missed it. It is not a hinder when one player hinders his partner.

Rule 4.11 - Avoidable Hinders. An avoidable hinder results in an "out" or a point depending upon whether the offender was serving or receiving.

(a) **Failure to Move.** Does not move sufficiently to allow opponent his shot.

(b) **Blocking.** Moves into a position effecting a block, on the opponent about to return the ball, or, in doubles, one partner moves in front of an opponent as his partner is returning the ball.

(c) **Moving into Ball.** Moves in the way and is struck by the ball just played by his opponent.

(d) **Pushing.** Deliberately pushing or shoving an opponent during a rally.

Rule 4.12 - Rest Periods. (a) Delays. Deliberate delay exceeding ten seconds by server, or receiver shall result in an out or point against the offender. (See Rule 4.1 (e).

(b) **During Game.** During a game each player in singles, or each side in doubles, either while serving or receiving may request a "time-out" for a towel, wiping glasses, change or adjustment. Each "time-out" shall not exceed 30 seconds. No more than three "time-outs" in a game shall be granted each singles players or each team in doubles. Two "time-outs" shall be allotted each player in singles or each team in doubles in the tie-breaker.

(c) **Injury.** No time shall be charged to a player who is injured during play. An injured player shall not be allowed more than a total of fifteen minutes of rest. If the injured player is not able to resume play after total rests of 15 minutes the match shall be awarded to the opponent or opponents. On any further injury to same player, the Tournament Director, if present, or committee after considering any available medical opinion shall determine whether the injured player will be allowed to continue.

(d) **Between Games.** A five minute rest period is allowed between the first and second games and a five minute rest period between the second and third games. Players may leave the court between games, but must be on the court and ready to play at the expiration of the rest period.

(e) Postponed Games. Any games postponed by referee due to weather elements shall be resumed with the same score as when postponed.

PART V. TOURNAMENTS

Rule 5.1 - Draws. The seeding method of drawing shall be the standard method approved by the U.S.R.A. and N.R.C. All draws in professional brackets shall be the responsibility of the National Director of the N.R.C.

Rule 5.2 - Scheduling. (a) Preliminary Matches. If one or more contestants are entered in both singles and doubles they may be required to play both singles and doubles on the same day or night with little rest between matches. This is a risk assumed on entering both singles and doubles. If possible the schedule should provide at least a one hour rest period between all matches.

(b) Final Matches. Where one or more players have reached the finals in both singles and doubles, it is recommended that the doubles match be played on the day preceding the singles. This would assume more rest between the final matches. If both final matches must be played on the same day or night, the following procedure should be followed:

(1) The singles match be played first.

(2) A rest period of not less than ONE HOUR be allowed between the finals in singles and doubles.

Rule 5.3 - Notice of Matches. After the first round of matches, it is the responsibility of each player to check the posted schedules to determine the time and place of each subsequent match. If any change is made in the schedule after posting, it shall be the duty of the committee or chairman to notify the players of the change.

Rule 5.4 - Third Place. In championship tournaments, national, state, district, etc. (if there is a playoff for third place), the loser in the semifinals must play for third place or lose his ranking for next year unless he is unable to compete because of injury or illness. See Rule 3.5 (d) (4).

Rule 5.5 U.S.R.A. Regional Tournaments. Each year the United States and Canada are divided into regions for the purpose of sectional competition preceding the National Championships. The exact boundaries of each region are dependent on the location of the regional tournaments. The locations are announced in NATIONAL RACQUETBALL magazine.

(a) Only players residing in the area defined can participate in a local tournament.

(b) Winners of open singles and ladies open singles in regional tournaments will receive round trip air coach tickets to the U.S.R.A. national tourney. Remuneration will be made after arrival at the Nationals.

(c) A U.S.R.A. officer will be in attendance at each regional tournament and will coordinate with the host chairman.

Awards: No individual award in U.S.R.A.-sanctioned tournaments should exceed value of more than $25.

Tournament Management: In all U.S.R.A.-sanctioned tournaments the tournament chairman and/or the national U.S.R.A. official in attendance may decide on a change of courts after the completion of any tournament game if such a change will accommodate better spectator conditions.

Tournament Conduct: In all U.S.R.A.-sanctioned tournaments the referee is empowered to default a match if an individual player or team conducts itself to the detriment of the tournament and the game.

Professional Definition: Any player who has accepted $1000 or more in prizes and/or prize money in the most recent 12 calendar months is considered a professional racquetball player and ineligible for participation in any U.S.R.A.-sanctioned tournament bracket.

Pick-A-Partner: The essence of the "Player's Fraternity" has been to allow player to come to tournaments and select a doubles partner, if necessary, regardless what organization or city he might represent.

Age Brackets: The following age brackets, determined by the age of the player on the first day of the tournament are:

Open: Any age can compete.

Juniors: 17 and under.

Seniors: 35 and over.

Masters: 45 and over.

Golden Masters: 55 and over.

In doubles both players must be within the specified age bracket.

THE UNITED STATES RACQUETBALL ASSOCIATION

The United States Racquetball Association (U.S.R.A.) was formed by Bob Kendler in 1973. The responsibility of the Association is to govern amateur racquetball in the United States.

The U.S.R.A. does many things behind the scenes for racquetball. It publishes the official rules of the game, publishes its magazine, *National Racquetball*, has affiliate organizations in every state, and sponsors amateur tournaments, from the National Championships to local events.

The U.S.R.A. rule book, which is free for all members, is a yearly publication giving all the rules and regulations under which the game is played. For a free copy contact your state association or the U.S.R.A.

National Racquetball, the monthly publication of the U.S.R.A. is the communications piece of the Association, your voice to what's going on within racquetball. *National Racquetball* is sectionalized to provide the subscriber with as much material on a variety of subjects within our sport as is possible.

U.S.R.A. affiliate organizations began with the work of Terry Fancher, the U.S.R.A.'s national coordinator, who spent a full year contacting various persons and organizations throughout the nation. Terry's goal, and that of the U.S.R.A. was to find capable people everywhere, who would volunteer their services to help organize racquetball on the state level.

Affiliates are encouraged to promote the sport in all areas, with special emphasis on junior and women players. Events sanctioned by state affiliates make them eligible for free balls, souvenir shirts, draw sheets, scorecards, rule books and other materials in the U.S.R.A.'s tournament package.

Two dollars of each subscription that comes into the U.S.R.A.'s treasury is re-imbursed to the to the states on a per membership basis. Over $100,000 has been "re-invested" in local racquetball by the U.S.R.A. through its affiliates in the past two years.

Many of the tournaments sponsored by the U.S.R.A. are of "major" title, including the National Championships in June each year, which culminates the Labor Day to Summer season.

Additionally, the Regional Championships fall under the jurisdiction of the U.S.R.A., which pays the full air fare round trip to the Nationals for all men and women open singles winners at the Regionals.

Every state championship is part of the U.S.R.A.'s far reaching program, as well as every local tournament sanctioned by the affiliates.

In all over 500 tournaments a year fall under the U.S.R.A.'s jurisdiction. That's plenty of racquetball, — for everyone.

The U.S.R.A. is an amateur organization, and sponsors only amateur tournaments, or the amateur brackets of play at a professional tournament. No player who has accepted $1000 or more in prize money in the past 12 months may play in U.S.R.A. events.

For further information on the United States Racquetball Association, contact the headquarters at 1101 Dempster Street, Skokie, Illinois 60076 or phone (312) 673-4000.